Praise
A Surgeon's Memoir

"Dr. Stewart Lazow provides an exceptional chronicle of his four decades as a 'County guy' at the Kings County Hospital Center in Brooklyn, New York, the very first level I trauma center (knife and gun club) in the United States. He takes us from the shooting in the oral surgery clinic with the three bullet holes in the cinderblock walls as a constant reminder, to the delirious pneumonia patient hurling his excrement (feces toss) at unsuspecting passersby in the A-11 inpatient ward. From buffoon rounds to arrow piercings to ice pick stabbings and coke bottles where they do not belong, not to mention the missing (stolen) blue Members Only jacket, Lazow both informs and entertains his readership with these stories as well as those about the County pain scale and the Spasm Dome. A must-read for all involved in the provision of graduate medical education at noteworthy, inner-city academic medical centers."

–**ERIC R. CARLSON**, DMD, MD, EdM, FACS, Professor and Kelly L. Krahwinkel Endowed Chairman, Department of Oral and Maxillofacial Surgery, University of Tennessee Graduate School of Medicine

"Having been there and lived through it, I still found myself laughing (and crying) while reading this book. For anyone under the impression that doctors just print money and golf, read this book, it will enlighten you!"

—**STEVEN IZZO**, DDS, Associate Director, Oral & Maxillofacial Surgery, Kings County Hospital, Brooklyn, NY

"*A Surgeon's Memoir* takes you in the moment you open the book. I traveled along his amazing trajectory enjoying every experience he related, both with humor, honesty, and humility. Each page was an adventure and insight into the world of Kings County Hospital Center in Brooklyn, NY, and the trials and tribulations Dr. Lazow encountered. A must-read!"

—**JOAN E. CHILDS**, LCSW, Psychotherapist, Author, Inspirational Speaker, Certified Life Coach, Relationship Coach, Trainer, Consultant

"Four decades in the making, from pencil to paper, and now in 206 pages, Dr. Lazow's book is a compelling read, both for those in the medical profession and ordinary people like me and you. Keep turning the pages and enjoy living vicariously through his memorable career moments."

—**SHARI COHEN**, Former Executive Director, Media Investments, Strategy & Innovation at WPP's GroupM

"If you have ever needed a doctor and wondered why their fees can be rather costly, read *40 Years at the County* and you will have new insight into the medical profession. Along with funny, crazy, and unbelievable anecdotes, you will learn of the extensive training and knowledge one needs to be an expert doctor/surgeon. Dr. Lazow's story is entertaining and educational. I highly recommend this deep dive into the education of a doctor and an enlightening journey through the halls of medicine."

—**JEROD RESNICK**, Retired NYC High School Principal

"The ultimate story of how an extern from Columbia became the King of the County. Cynical and sarcastic through and through. A thrilling ride from cover to cover."

—**ROMAN TEMKIN**, DDS, Former Kings County Hospital OMS Chief Resident

A Surgeon's Memoir:
40 Years at the County
by Stewart K. Lazow, MD, DDS, FACS

© Copyright 2024 Stewart K Lazow, MD, DDS, FACS

ISBN 979-8-88824-307-7

Published by

köehlerbooks™

3705 Shore Drive
Virginia Beach, VA 23455
800-435-4811
www.koehlerbooks.com

A SURGEON'S MEMOIR:

40 Years at the County

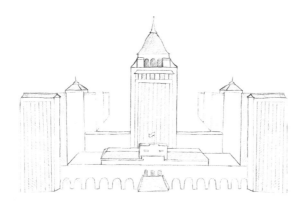

STEWART K. LAZOW,

MD, DDS, FACS (retired)

VIRGINIA BEACH
CAPE CHARLES

To my wife, Helaine, for her enduring support.

To my children, Margot, Stefanie, and Zachary—
I live vicariously through your accomplishments.

To my residents who constantly pushed
the envelope and kept me young.

Ground Rules

1. Colleagues' names are mentioned when appropriate and with their permission.

2. Patient identities are protected to maintain privacy and ensure HIPAA compliance.

3. Resident names are excluded to protect the innocent and not so innocent.

4. Vignettes are accurate accounts only as far as memory and poetic license allow.

Contents

Foreword

ARMED WITH A TALL GLASS of Jameson Irish Whiskey over ice, I sat down in my swivel-rocker wicker chair and lit the fire pit. As I puffed on my ever-present pipe, it suddenly hit me:

I have a story to tell.

September 2018, I tuned in to watch a popular new medical drama. Just what we needed— another in a plethora of medical shows. Five minutes into the story, I blurted to my wife, "OMG, it's the County." Although the television show is supposedly based at Bellevue Hospital, several of the scenes were filmed at my old stomping grounds, Kings County Hospital Center, in Brooklyn, New York. The County is to Brooklyn what Bellevue is to Manhattan, both massive inner-city public teaching hospitals.

After fast-forwarding through the episode—does anyone really watch the commercials anymore?—I retreated to the lanai. I must admit life's not too tough here in beautiful Naples, Florida. I had just turned sixty-five the very day I retired. I was in reasonably good health, albeit a dozen or so pounds overweight, and sporting the same salt-and-pepper beard for as long as I could dare to remember.

During my forty-year journey, culminating as professor, vice chairman, Oral and Maxillofacial Surgery (OMS) residency program director, and director of service at Kings County Hospital Center, I'd seen it all. I witnessed countless patient encounters—some comical, some tragic, some that confirmed my faith in the human spirit—in addition to shocking resident foibles. I had my share of rewarding cases as well as heartbreaking failures.

I fought my share of "turf wars." I withstood an ever-increasing aggravation quotient from every acronym known to man, including

HIPAA, JCAHO, CODA, and my personal favorite, the EHR (all will be defined hence). I'd become utterly dismayed by a fractured, grossly inefficient healthcare delivery system. Simply stated, healthcare spending per capita in the United States is twice that of our peer developed nations.

The County certainly isn't for everyone. I guess I was just a "County" guy.

Prologue

REWIND TO 1978. It was a typically hot, humid Monday morning in late June. My co-extern and I walked from the ivory towers of Columbia Presbyterian Medical Center toward the subway station at 168th Street and Broadway. We had lost the oral surgery externship lottery for the summer between our third and fourth year at Columbia School of Dental and Oral Surgery. No Columbia, Cornell, Mount Sinai, Long Island Jewish, or NYU for us. Instead, Dr. Louis Mandel (aka Sweet Lou), the patriarch of oral surgery at Columbia, had exiled us to Kings County Hospital. The County, as it was known to the four million denizens of Brooklyn, was the New York City Health and Hospitals Corporation (NYCHHC) equivalent of Bellevue in Manhattan.

At six thirty a.m., with trepidation, we began the ninety-minute subway trek into the bowels of Brooklyn. We hopped onto the #1 local heading downtown and picked up the express at 96th Street. We switched to the #5 train at Bowling Green, the southern tip of Manhattan, for the trip into Brooklyn. The subway car was hot without air conditioning. No seats were available. It was particularly malodorous as the straphangers were packed in like sardines.

We exited the subway at the Winthrop Avenue station onto East Flatbush. We walked south on Nostrand Avenue among a sea of humanity all apparently heading to Kings County, the largest employer in Brooklyn. After a quick left onto Clarkson Avenue, the three majestic towers of the A, B, and C buildings of the hospital came into view. The B building was the second tallest structure in Brooklyn at the time, while the downtown Williamsburgh Savings Bank was the tallest. Sweating profusely in the hot sun, we proceeded past the medical school at Downstate Medical Center and University Hospital across the street to the south. We entered the B building through the impressive marble entrance past the original cornerstone laid in 1831.

In fact, the roots of Kings County were planted in central Brooklyn in 1830, when a 200-acre parcel of land was purchased for $3,000 to build a one-room public infirmary for the sick. The Department of Oral Surgery, established in 1926, was one of the first of its kind in the United States.

After navigating the labyrinth of the B building ground floor, we entered the Oral Surgery Clinic. It looked like a dungeon, with three bullet holes in the cinderblock walls of the crowded waiting room. Upon our persistent inquiry, the receptionist reluctantly recounted the infamous prisoner escape from the clinic in the spring of 1975. An inmate from the Brooklyn House of Detention, aka the Big House, had concocted his getaway along the lines of Michael Corleone's famous planted gun scene in the bathroom in *The Godfather*. A week earlier, the inmate had undergone a difficult tooth extraction in the clinic. Evidently, he had done his homework. Three days post-op, he complained of exquisite pain consistent with a "dry socket," or alveolitis, requiring daily socket dressing changes. On the third post-op visit to the clinic, he asked the guard if he could use the restroom. It was small and could only accommodate one person. Like the scene in *The Godfather*, the prisoner's girlfriend had already planted a gun in the stall. He came out guns blazing, killing one cop and critically injuring another, shot a patient, and left three bullet holes eternally in the cinderblock. He fled in his girlfriend's waiting vehicle.

Following this introduction, we were then whisked to the back of the clinic to meet with the dental department chairman. I thought I was presentable for our orientation, neatly attired in pressed khaki pants, Izod shirt, and new Adidas sneakers. I extended my hand to introduce myself. No welcoming handshake was offered in return. Instead, the baldheaded chair defiantly blurted, "Go home. Return tomorrow dressed professionally or not at all." And so began my forty years at the County.

Extern 1978

EXTERNSHIP AT THE COUNTY was great. If you were aggressive and reliable, you were allowed to perform a myriad of minor oral surgical procedures—routine extractions, removal of easy impacted wisdom teeth, biopsies, and alveoplasties (bone trim)—all under resident supervision of course. It was like being an intern without the real responsibility of the interns. Minimal scut work—writing notes and orders, patient transport, dressing changes, blood draws, and starting IVs—was the domain of the interns. On-call for externs was voluntary, only once a week compared to being on-call every third day (q3) for the interns. On-call offered an excellent opportunity to practice suturing techniques of facial lacerations and was generally worth it.

Every day, morning rounds began at seven a.m. before clinic or the OR (on Mondays and Fridays). This meant hitting the subway by five thirty. Evening rounds started at five p.m. or later—tea time as the residents affectionately called it. We would all gather in the dingy resident room, drinking coffee and smoking cigarettes. We waited for the last patient straggler to be treated in the clinic before all going together on inpatient rounds in the main hospital. Rounding on patients with facial fractures, benign head and neck tumors, or major orofacial infections provided a wealth of clinical material unlike anything I had seen in dental school.

At lunchtime every Thursday, we had grand rounds with the program director (PD) and chair. While a bit unnerving, it offered the interns an opportunity to present the cases of the week. The program director routinely asked them about everything from interpreting lab values, reading chest X-rays, and deciphering electrocardiograms (EKGs). It was all new to my co-extern and me, but in the rare moments that we actually knew the answer when the interns didn't, we shined. Roundsmanship it was called.

After completing our six-week externship, my colleague and I had become respected team members because we had lightened the interns' workload. We presented cases on daily rounds and even on grand rounds, though with some hesitation. We scrubbed in and assisted in the OR. Therefore, for our last clinic session, our two benevolent chief residents (CRs) threw each of us a bone. We were each allowed to perform a more advanced elective oral surgical procedure. I scheduled an anterior maxillary apicoectomy—a surgical root canal. Midway through it, my CR poked his head into the operatory. Noticing blood all over the mayo stand, he pulled me aside. He said, "Fella, isn't it better than sex?" "Maybe for you it is," I replied. I was hooked . . . and the patient survived.

After the County externship, my senior year of dental school was anticlimactic. The externship, with its confluence of medicine, surgery, and dentistry, had confirmed my desire to pursue an oral surgery residency. I therefore loaded up on oral surgery electives at Columbia affiliates, including Harlem Hospital, Mount Sinai Hospital, and the Bronx VA Hospital.

The Bronx VA rotation was memorable for one patient encounter with a World War II veteran with a forty pack-year smoking history. He presented with a fungating soft tissue mass in the floor of his mouth. Somewhat intimidated, I presented this case of obvious stage four squamous cell carcinoma to the oral surgery service chief. He was a distinguished European-trained dual-degree surgeon with head and neck fellowship training. The surgeon formally introduced himself to the terrified patient, saying, "I have good news and bad news for you. The bad news is you have cancer. The good news is I'm here to operate on you." Indeed, this was a truly remarkable example of a surgeon's hubris.

It was soon time for me to apply to oral surgery residency programs. In 1978-79, the oral surgery residency application process totally favored the residency programs. In contrast, the current OMS match process skewed to the applicants was still years away. Today, the National Match handles more than 450 applications annually to fill roughly 200 OMS categorical positions in a fair and unpressured manner, with a 45 percent acceptance rate into the highly competitive specialty.

I interviewed at over a half dozen New York programs. In fact, I had only applied to New York programs. Unexpectedly, my father had passed away, on his fifty-fourth birthday, during my first year of dental school in 1976—right in the middle of my gross anatomy course, no less. The autopsy was inconclusive but suggestive of carbon tetrachloride poisoning. This probably resulted from many nights spent in his poorly ventilated basement workshop, working on his recently patented golf tee invention. He was hospitalized and kept alive in a coma for several weeks. Inexplicably, he awoke from his month-long coma on Christmas day to remind me to take care of my mother and sister when he was gone. This was a commitment I would honor for the next thirty-six years until my mother passed away in 2012. It would influence several career decisions I would make in the future.

On the evening of December 28, I received a call from the chairman of the Kings County Hospital program offering me the position. Yes, this was the same person who had kicked me out on the first day of my externship. It was a take it or leave it proposition. Through the grapevine, I had become aware that I was the first alternate at three other fine programs. However, there was no time for me to check out my options. After all, despite its ambience, the County offered a wealth of unsurpassed clinical experience. I knew that I would treat cases at the County that I wouldn't see anywhere else. I gratefully accepted the position on the spot. Later, I found out that thanks to the recommendations of the two chief residents and program director, the department had broken precedence in accepting both my co-extern and me into the program.

Intern Year

DAY 1

Intern year started with a bang on Sunday, July 1, 1979. Armed with my extern experience, I was granted the ignominious task of taking the first on-call assignment. Little did I know that day we would set a record still on the books some forty years later.

I arrived somewhat anxious and apprehensive in the B building resident room at seven a.m. I was nattily attired in my new, pressed white pants, green scrub shirt, and short white lab jacket with the Kings County Hospital insignia on the left shoulder. It would still be another year before residents were granted long white coats to distinguish them from medical students who wore short jackets. By eight a.m., my new pager, which I would soon come to detest, summoned me stat to the C-1 acute trauma section of the emergency department. Fortunately, the entire on-call team, including the newly minted chief residents and one junior resident, was still rounding on our inherited inpatients from the previous regime. Upon arrival in the emergency room, it became obvious that there were two trauma victims with severe facial injuries. Since it was the first of the month, all maxillofacial trauma that day was handled by the oral and maxillofacial surgery service.

EMS brought in the two patients, White males in their twenties. The driver and the front seat passenger had been involved in a high-speed motor vehicle versus light pole accident. Unrestrained, apparently they had struck their faces on the dashboard and windshield. The trauma general surgery resident running the C-1 area reported that both patients presented with a Glasgow Coma Scale score of 8 (GCS, see Appendix I), warranting intubation to secure their airways. Cervical collars were already placed in the field by EMS pending

C-spine clearance. The men were moderately hypotensive on arrival but responded well to aggressive fluid resuscitation. Chest, abdomen, pelvis, and extremity workup was surprisingly negative. Head CT was negative for intracranial bleed or shift. Facial CT revealed multiple facial fractures in both patients. Appropriate consultations and clearances were obtained from neurosurgery, ophthalmology, and trauma surgery. Lab values were essentially normal, including surprisingly negative blood alcohol levels in both cases. Epistaxis was controlled by nasal packing. Facial lacerations were temporarily closed with stay sutures pending definitive plastic closure in the OR. Medical histories and consents were obtained from both patients' families, who had arrived in the ER, escorted by police. The patients were cleared and stable for surgery.

The maxillofacial injuries were almost identical. Both patients presented with grossly mobile maxillary (upper jaw) LeFort III and mandible (lower jaw) fractures. This was record setting! To this day forty years later, my very first day on-call was the only time two LeFort III fractures were admitted on the same day. René LeFort, a French surgeon in 1901, had classified midface fracture patterns (Appendix II) by dropping cadaver skulls from the ceiling of his anatomy lab to the floor. He created a classification scheme with three types of fractures. As the classification increases, the anatomical level and severity of the midfacial fracture ascends from inferior to superior. LeFort I is a horizontal maxillary fracture above the roots of the upper teeth. LeFort II is a midfacial pyramidal fracture. LeFort III is a complete craniofacial disjunction of the midface involving the nasal bones, orbits (eye socket), and zygomas (cheekbone). It is the most severe of the midfacial fractures, involving the greatest impact force.

We decided to operate on one of the patients that evening and schedule the other for repair during our usual Monday morning OR block time. I spent that first day running blood tests to and from the lab, as well as type and crossing the patients to make sure blood products were available during surgery.

My chief residents and junior resident, along with our program director, who happened to be the emergency attending on-call, spent the entire night in the OR performing an open reduction and internal fixation (ORIF) of the LeFort III and mandible fractures. I was therefore left alone in the ER, totally green except for my externship experience, suturing facial lacerations all night long. I never stopped to eat; sleeping was out of the question.

By seven a.m., when the whole new-day team arrived for a.m. rounds, I was exhausted and yet strangely exhilarated. It was time to run the clinic along with my co-intern while the rest of the team operated on LeFort III #2. After my thirty-five-hour nonstop session, I was finally excused to go home at six p.m. I exited the hospital glancing over my shoulder at the ER ambulance bay, changed forever. I was on my way to becoming an oral surgeon.

SPLAT

Intern year is the most challenging and demanding year of a resident's life, mentally and physically. In 1979, there was no Bell Commission and subsequent adoption of its 405 regulations, limiting resident on-duty hours to twenty-four hours per shift and eighty hours per week. The infamous Libby Zion case, which claimed resident malpractice due to exhaustion and lack of attending supervision, at New York Hospital, was still five years in the future. OMS interns were routinely on-call every third night; a thirty-six-hour shift was commonplace. We worked all night suturing lacerations in the ER, admitting fracture and infection patients, and taking care of inpatients on the wards. Then we would work in the busy clinic the next day. Clinic was both demanding and repetitive. Often, as many as eighty oral surgery patients were treated by three residents for pre-operative evaluation, post-operative follow-up, and minor oral surgery procedures. To earn a "golden weekend off," the interns would have to work a sixty-hour shift from Saturday seven a.m. till Monday seven p.m. once a month.

Accommodations were suboptimal at best. Rather than taking advantage of our designated on-call room in the main hospital, most of us opted to sleep on clean sheets on the recovery room cot in the clinic immediately adjacent to the ER. ENT (ear, nose, and throat) handled all the maxillofacial trauma every Monday. One quiet Monday night on-call after a vacation in Florida, I had just dozed off when my beeper blared at three a.m. Startled, I awoke to see a giant cockroach crawling across my chest. I totally freaked out and didn't sleep again the rest of that shift.

Midway through the year, our Committee of Interns and Residents staged a strike, demanding improved workplace conditions. It seemed like a worthwhile concept until Mayor Ed Koch invoked the Taft Hartley Act. By doing so, he classified us as essential government employees, docking us two days' pay for every day out on the picket line. The work stoppage halted immediately.

Intern year was equally challenging academically. Blood tests, chest X-rays, EKGs, facial X-rays, and CT scans all required analysis and interpretation. We were forced to audit a rigorous physical diagnosis course at Downstate Medical College with first-year med students. This course would eventually credential us to perform the required admission history and physical for each of our inpatients. Of course, in 1980, a real MD still had to co-sign them. Interestingly enough, Dr. Bombay, not the infamous character on the TV series *Bewitched*, just happened to illegibly co-sign most of our H&Ps that year. Our off-service rotations, including four months in total on both anesthesia and internal medicine, came as a welcome respite to the monotony of the oral surgery service. But they also presented new and unique challenges of their own to those of us uninitiated in those medical fields.

My medicine rotation provided me with the most memorable experience of the intern year. My co-intern and I were both assigned to the medicine service on the A-11 inpatient ward at the County, essentially functioning as sub-interns. Two sub-intern rotators were expected to handle the workload of one medicine intern. We treated a garden variety of routine medical conditions—diabetes, asthma, emphysema, hypertension, heart disease, liver disease, kidney disease . . .

While on-call one hot June overnight, we were joined at the nurses' station by the graveyard shift crew—the head nurse, another RN, and two LPNs—for our usual four a.m. coffee and donuts. Suddenly, a particularly hideous scent wafted in from the sixteen-bed main ward. We donned facemasks. Much to our collective dismay, we witnessed the patient in bed number three, a middle-aged Black man admitted with a diagnosis of pneumonia, sitting upright and tossing human excrement at unsuspecting sleeping patients across the room. SPLAT! INCOMING! Trying to reason with him was futile; we called security. The hospital police could barely restrain him physically as he seemed to possess supernatural powers at that moment. A stat psychiatry consult was requested.

Thirty minutes later, the bespectacled psych resident arrived. Half-asleep, he looked at the scene. By now, the staff and patients were all wearing masks. He never requested one for himself. Nonchalantly, he assessed the situation. "Feces toss," he declared. He walked to the nurses' station and calmly ordered enough Thorazine (generic-chlorpromazine), the antipsychotic of choice in those days, to sedate an elephant. He triumphantly turned and walked to the elevator.

Junior Year

BUFFOON ROUNDS

My junior resident year began with a brief orientation for the new interns from the chair, OMS program director, and GPR program director. Six OMS residents plus two general practice dental residents (GPRs-See Cheat Sheet at the back of the book) met in the resident room in the B building ground floor clinic at seven a.m. and embarked on a hospital tour.

We proceeded to the surgical intensive care unit (SICU) after brief stops in the ER and on our B-51/52 inpatient wards. In Room #1, I presented the patient's medical and surgical history to the assembled group. This was a severely injured, intubated polytrauma patient whom we had operated on the previous Friday to reduce and fixate his midface and mandible fractures. The new CR directed me to draw an arterial blood gas to assess the patient's oxygenation in anticipation of possible extubation. Since the patient was acutely edematous and with fractures of both upper extremities, I had no choice but to perform a femoral stick. I prepped his right groin with alcohol and palpated his femoral artery. Using an eighteen-gauge needle on a 10cc syringe, I advanced the needle to the hub in the inguinal crease until I noticed pulsatile bright-red blood return in the syringe. I drew back 10 cc of arterial blood, removed the needle from the groin, and put pressure on the puncture site to prevent hematoma formation.

I heard a thud. One of the newly minted GPRs, fresh out of dental school, had passed out, hitting his rather large noggin on the floor. The chair, in his infinite wisdom, commanded us to sit him up. But we needed to increase the blood flow to his brain rather than decrease it, so our OMS program director overruled him. We placed the GPR in Trendelenburg position, with his head down and legs elevated. He awakened with a wet paper towel on his forehead, fortunately not bleeding, with no palpable skull fracture nor neurological deficit.

We exited the SICU totally embarrassed, the OMS service having been set back twenty years by the general dentists. So was born the tradition of buffoon rounds.

GA ROOM

Junior year meant another two months on the anesthesia service at the County, honing my airway and intubation skills. I also became familiar with the medications (brand name/generic name) that I would be using in our ambulatory general anesthesia (GA) suite, such as Valium (diazepam-sedative), Demerol (meperidine-narcotic), Brevital (methohexital-general anesthetic), and Fluothane (halothane-inhalation agent). Sidebar: Over time, better pharmaceutical agents, such as Versed (midazolam), Sublimaze (fentanyl), Diprivan (propofol), and Ultane (sevoflurane) would replace those medications.

Quickly, I realized that if I did the pre-op and post-op evaluations and set up the OR, the anesthetist I was assigned to work with would let me run the case under her supervision.

With four months of anesthesia training in the OR to my credit, I was now deemed eligible to administer general anesthesia in the GA room, located in the back of our clinic, on Tuesday, Wednesday, and Thursday. This was of course under attending supervision, while the chief residents performed more advanced office oral surgical procedures under general anesthesia, such as difficult impacted wisdom teeth and closed reductions of mandible fractures.

Nicknamed the "Spasm Dome" because of the high incidence of laryngospasms associated with the short-acting barbiturate Brevital, the GA room was a respite from the daily monotony of the busy local anesthetic-driven clinic. Laryngospasm, or inability to ventilate the patient through blocked vocal cords, was disconcerting to the novice anesthetist. But it never unnerved my program director, Dr. Bernard

Gold, who was an exodontist/anesthetist icon. Outside his legendary private practice on Pitkin Avenue in Brooklyn, the patients would line up at eight a.m. If they could walk up the steep staircase to his second-floor office, they were deemed suitable candidates for general anesthesia. Routinely, he performed forty GAs per day and was finished by two p.m. His senior partner could perform a full mouth extraction case (thirty-two teeth) under GA with only one carpule of local anesthesia and a single suture in twenty minutes.

In the midst of a full-blown laryngospasm, with the patient turning blue (this was before mandatory pulse oximetry monitoring), Dr. Gold would announce to anyone listening that "laryngospasm doesn't raise my BP more than ten mm Hg." If positive pressure ventilation with oxygen via full face mask didn't break the spasm in thirty seconds, then twenty milligrams of Anectine (succinylcholine-a depolarizing neuromuscular blocking agent or paralytic) was administered intravenously. Of course, then you had to ventilate the patient until he started to breathe on his own again. To prevent possible bradycardia (low pulse rate) after repeated doses of succinylcholine, Dr. Gold routinely administered atropine (atropine sulfate) to all his GA patients pre-operatively. But this was not without risk and could cause atropine toxicity, with the patient becoming "red as a beet, dry as a bone, and crazy as a loon." At least we got a publication out of it. Having performed more than 600 ambulatory GAs annually, we all became proficient anesthetists upon completion of the residency.

KNIFE AND GUN CLUB

Unlike heroin, which was relatively sedating, crack cocaine caused a marked increase in violent crime in New York City. The epidemic that was just starting in inner-city neighborhoods led to a dramatic increase in penetrating trauma patients inundating the trauma team at the County.

Kings County had been named the very first Level I trauma center in the country. The Army routinely sent its trauma surgeons and medics to train at the County before deploying them overseas. In 1980, the violence along Eastern Parkway at the annual West Indian Labor Day Parade sent a record forty-seven gunshot and stabbing victims to the County ER. So, the Kings County Knife and Gun Club was born.

Besides the onslaught of penetrating trauma, we also saw the typical high-speed motor vehicle accidents, fractures, and burns. Eighteen admissions a night was commonplace. Eighty patients might be on the service on any given day. It was a physically demanding but exhilarating rotation.

It was a great era for an oral surgery resident to rotate on the trauma service, which was run by general surgery. The two-month trauma rotation, followed by an additional month in the SICU, was the highlight of the junior resident year.

The trauma team was composed of an indomitable general surgery chief resident who virtually never left the hospital during his mandatory six-week rotation, two third-year senior surgical residents who were on-call every other night, and three surgical interns on-call every third night. I functioned as a surgery intern along with a fourth-year extern from Chicago and three third-year medical students from SUNY Downstate. The fourth-year extern, a surgery wannabe, was aggressive and quite competent.

The chief and senior residents operated around the clock. The medical students who rotated with me every third night confirmed the eleventh law of Samuel Shem's infamous 1978 treatise, *The House of God*: "Show me a medical student who only triples my work and I will kiss his feet."

Having shown interest and a modicum of surgical aptitude, I quickly had my own mini-trauma team, composed of me, the extern, and the three medical students. We rounded on the typical eighty patient census housed on the C11 and C12 trauma wards and boarded all over the hospital. We handled all scut work during the day, including admissions, discharges, progress notes (handwritten in those days and mostly illegible), dressing changes, IVs, blood draws, consults, and trauma transport to radiology for CT scans. But night-time was when all hell broke loose.

WTF/HOW AM I DOING?

Looking back, the most interesting aspects of my residency were my WTF moments.

One October night, while the rest of the team was busy in the OR with two gunshot wound (GSW) victims, I experienced my first WTF moment. Two New York City cops were involved in a high-speed chase with a crack dealer when a minivan T-boned the police cruiser, hurling it into a light pole on Ocean Parkway. EMS routinely took all injured police and firemen to the County, the NYCHHC Level I trauma center for all of Brooklyn. In the C-1 acute trauma area, at midnight we received a heads-up that EMS had scooped up the officers and were ten minutes away. I called up to the OR to advise the team of the expected blunt trauma victims. I was emphatically directed to "man up, and deal with it."

Upon arrival, both White males in their thirties were conscious and hemodynamically stable but visibly traumatized. I followed the acute blunt trauma protocol. Primary assessment including airway, breathing, and cardiovascular were all stable. The secondary survey was clinically negative. GCS-15 was assigned as both patients were neurologically intact. I placed two large bore peripheral IVs in each patient and administered fluids. I ordered cervical spine films (C-collars had been placed in the field), CT head scans, and chest X-rays. The patients' pelvises were stable and no obvious extremity fractures were noted.

Although the abdomen was clinically benign in each case, we had to perform a diagnostic peritoneal lavage (DPL) to rule out intraab-dominal bleeding. Sidebar: Abdominal/pelvic CT and FAST (focused assessment with sonography for trauma) were not yet the standard of care. With an absence of obvious facial fractures, I passed a nasogastric tube in each patient to decompress the abdomen. Without evidence of urethral bleed or scrotal hematoma, I placed a Foley catheter to decompress the bladder.

The DPL was an invasive procedure with rare but significant potential morbidity. I had already performed multiple DPLs but always with senior resident supervision. Well, at the County it's "see one, do one, teach one." So, I consulted the surgery attending covering the C-1 area. "Go for it; call me if you need me," he said as he returned to his on-call room. I performed a semi-open DPL technique with a small vertical midline infra-umbilical incision. I inserted an eighteen-gauge needle at a forty-five-degree angle with two audible pops as it pierced the fascia and peritoneum. A Seldinger technique was used to pass the catheter into the peritoneal cavity toward the pelvis. Lactated Ringer's solution was infused into the abdomen, then subsequently aspirated five minutes later. Both specimens were grossly negative for blood and were then sent to the lab for microscopic analysis.

Fortunately, both DPLs were negative without evidence of intraabdominal bleed nor injury to the bladder or gastrointestinal tract. All labs, X-rays, and CT scans were within normal limits. I packaged up both patients and sent them upstairs to the VIP suite, which I didn't even know existed until the overnight administrator clued me in.

By three a.m., relieved and somewhat proud of myself, I paused for coffee and a cigarette in the nurses' lounge. Yes, everyone on the trauma team smoked in those days to deal with the stress. Suddenly, the C-1 head nurse came running in to get me. She looked like she had just seen a ghost. Apparently, Mayor Ed Koch was on the phone. As mayor, he was in charge of the entire NYCHHC, including Kings County Hospital. He wanted to speak to the trauma surgeon who had treated two of New York's finest. WTF! This was the very same mayor who traveled around the city asking New Yorkers, "How am I doing?" Somewhat shaken, I grabbed the phone and assured him that the policemen were stable and admitted overnight for observation. He thanked me for my expert care and advised that he would see the patients first thing in the morning.

Sure enough, Mayor Koch and his aides stormed into the VIP suite as we were rounding on the cops at eight a.m. The surgery department chairman, the trauma service director at the County, the County CEO, and the entire resident team, including me, greeted them. Having been up all night, I was exhausted and looked terrible.

The chief resident called upon me to present the cases. Fortunately, the cops were awake, alert, and anxious to be discharged. They graciously thanked me for my care and concern. The mayor asked my name and shook my hand as he exited. As the chairman turned to leave, I overheard him ask the CR who the hell I was since he didn't recognize me as one of his general surgery residents. When advised that I was an oral surgery rotator, he shook his head and muttered, "What the fuck?" The mayor never knew that two of New York City's finest had been treated by an oral surgeon.

WTF/JUNK

One Saturday, just after midnight during my trauma rotation, EMS brought in a thirty-year-old Black female, scantily clad, with a single GSW to the groin area. Hemodynamically stable, she was screaming at the top of her lungs for pain meds, flailing all four extremities. Once again, I was alone running the C-1 area; the rest of the trauma team was busy running two ORs. Suddenly, hysterical screams burst from the well-trained, experienced nurses, who had pulled the curtain to remove her garments with a modicum of privacy. WTF. *She* had a *penis*—a prodigious one at that. Miraculously, the bullet had missed all vital structures, leaving only a superficial graze wound to the penis and upper thigh.

During the examination, it became obvious that the patient had begun gender reassignment surgery. Having undergone feminizing augmentation mammoplasty (boob job), facial feminization cosmetic surgery, and reduction thyroid chondroplasty (tracheal shave), she was saving her money to proceed with definitive, though expensive, vaginoplasty.

It was 1980, twelve years before *The Crying Game*, the British thriller with a surprise transgender twist. A transvestite, transgender, or transsexual patient was still an enigma to us all. IV fluids, antibiotics, and a tetanus shot were administered, and a urology consult was obtained.

It was now time to transfer the patient to the floor for overnight observation. The patient requested to be admitted to the C-12 female trauma ward. This was met with instant resistance from their nursing staff after admission history and examination led to the discovery of her penis. When the patient was shuttled to the all-male C-11 ward, she was greeted with catcalls and whistles. Confronted with this dilemma, the overnight hospital administrator admitted the patient to the VIP suite for a one-night stay.

~

Two weeks later, EMS brought in an obviously psychotic twenty-two-year-old White male to the C-1 trauma area. Bleeding profusely from the groin, he was moderately hypotensive and tachycardic, conscious but clearly delirious, screaming obscenities to no one in particular. Upon stripping off his blood-soaked jeans and briefs, I was dumbfounded to see the shaft of his penis still barely attached by his urethra to the base. Suffering from auditory hallucinations, he heard voices emanating from his genitalia. These voices apparently led him to attempt to sever his penis, which was hanging by a thread.

Quickly, I applied a pressure dressing, started two large bore IVs, and administered fluids to correct his hypotension. A stat urology consult was called. A stat psych consult was obviously in order.

The urology and psych residents arrived almost simultaneously. The psych resident asked the patient if he still heard voices coming from his penis. The patient claimed that he heard them louder than ever. Before staff rushed him up to the OR to reattach his penis, the urology resident removed the dressing to examine the extent of the penile injury. The psych resident nearly passed out.

~

As the low man on the on-call totem pole, I was assigned to work on Thanksgiving Day. Thanksgiving is always a busy day in the G building psych ER, but it was a slow trauma day; that is until the trauma team was paged stat for an acute abdomen, interrupting our turkey dinner in the cafeteria. On arrival in the C-1 trauma area, we saw a thin mid-twenties Hispanic male in acute distress. Hypotensive and tachycardic, his abdomen was obviously distended with rebound tenderness throughout. Bowel sounds were muffled. I started two large bore peripheral IVs to administer fluids and sent off a full set of labs, including liver function tests and amylase. A stool guaiac was grossly positive for fecal occult blood. An abdominal X-ray series was ordered. I was assigned the trauma transport duty of accompanying him to radiology down the hall. I had no sooner returned with the patient to the C-1 bay when the radiology resident frantically called, summoning the trauma team to the reading room. The radiograph was on the view box; X-rays don't lie. Plain as day, we could all see the silhouette of a Coke bottle having passed the rectum superiorly into the lower sigmoid colon. With a little imagination, we could make out the cursive script of a Coca-Cola glass bottle.

When questioned further, the patient would only admit to having accidentally sat on the bottle. Attempts to retrieve it transanally were unsuccessful and excruciatingly painful for all involved. Now totally obstructed, the patient was taken emergently to the OR for an exploratory laparotomy.

SECOND CALL

After completing my trauma rotation, I was deemed fully ready, willing, and able to assume second-call responsibilities. My fellow junior and chief residents were more than happy to vouch for my capability to ascend the graduated level of resident responsibility. It was not so much for my newfound competence; I was a welcome addition to the junior roster to minimize their own second-call schedule.

Second call had its pluses and minuses. The good news—no more in-house on-calls. I was now free to sleep in my own bed at night but with my trusty long-range beeper on my night table, dreading that two a.m. page. The bad news—the added responsibility for each admission. Each overnight facial fracture, serious orofacial infection, or major laceration required the second call to perform a history and physical before seven a.m. rounds. If the injury was severe enough or the patient was unstable, the two a.m. drive through the bowels of Brooklyn back to the County could be harrowing. It was like driving in a third world country with little or no respect for red lights or stop signs.

Courtesy of the Kings County Knife and Gun Club, while on second call, the EMS brought in a twenty-eight-year-old Black male with an ice pick embedded up to the handle in his right orbit. It entered immediately superior to and medial to the globe. Conscious and stable, albeit hysterical, the patient's vision in passive gaze was grossly normal. His extraocular movements revealed pronounced limitation in right lateral and inferior gaze due to impingement by the ice pick. He claimed to have been stabbed in a drug deal gone bad.

Facial films and head CT confirmed a six-inch stiletto blade that had bypassed his globe, piercing the right superior medial orbital wall at the lesser wing of the sphenoid bone. It miraculously missed the optic nerve and ophthalmic artery while penetrating the skull base. Stat ophthalmology and neurosurgery consults were obtained. A cerebral angiogram, not without its inherent stroke risk, was performed to rule out intracranial vascular injury. Sidebar: This was the era long before magnetic resonance angiography and CT angiography were available, so the angiogram was in order.

All studies were surprisingly negative. The patient was taken to the OR by the OMS service with ophtho and neurosx on standby. The ice pick was atraumatically removed with only moderate resistance. No major bleeding was encountered. The patient was admitted for overnight observation to rule out intracranial bleed or CSF leak. No change in vision or neuro status was observed. Extraocular movements were much improved.

We all held our collective breath for an injury that could leave him blind, neurologically impaired, or dead. Miraculously, he walked out of the hospital the very next day with appointments for routine follow-up. Go figure.

~

One late night in early spring of 1981, while on second call, the on-call intern summoned me urgently to the County for a penetrating traumatic facial wound. When I arrived in the C-1 area, I couldn't believe my eyes.

A twenty-year-old White male had seemingly copied Steve Martin's Wild and Crazy Guys *Saturday Night Live* routine with a through-and-through arrow piercing the right cheek and exiting his left cheek. He was conscious and hemodynamically stable without an expanding hematoma associated with the facial arteries. He was neurologically intact with no facial nerve deficits bilaterally. Unfortunately, the arrow had transected the ventral surface of the tongue at the junction of its anterior two-thirds and posterior one-third. There was no brisk hemorrhage from the lingual arteries, nor an expanding hematoma in the floor of the mouth associated with the lingual veins. Bilateral angiography could not be justified in this case by the apparent track of the penetrating trauma anterior to the carotids.

Without consulting my third-call chief resident for fear of waking him at three a.m., I slowly and atraumatically removed the arrow under mild sedation in the C-1 area with the trauma team on standby. I encountered no major bleeding, and the airway was unobstructed. The hypoglossal and lingual nerves to the tongue appeared grossly intact. After vigorous irrigation, I sutured both cheek wounds in layers. I sutured the entrance wound to the right side of the tongue and packed open the exit wound of the left ventral tongue, obliterating any midglossal dead space. The patient tolerated the procedure well and was kept in the trauma bay for airway observation, IV antibiotics, and a tetanus shot before being transferred to another area at six a.m.

I was feeling pretty proud of myself as I recounted the case to my whole team as we set off on morning rounds. We arrived at the patient's bed on our B-51 oral surgery ward to find his bedside curtains drawn. I pulled the curtains back to a loud group gasp. We found him sitting upright in his bed, intuitively to protect his airway.

His tongue was now grossly edematous and so swollen in his open mouth that it resembled a salami. An onslaught of pimping questions from my chief residents ensued: "Why hadn't I contacted third call? Why didn't I have anesthesia nasally intubate him to secure the airway?" We rushed him to the surgical ICU for airway observation with a trach set at bedside.

Steroids, a bit after the fact, helped with the swelling somewhat. Despite my inexperience, his glossal edema gradually resolved. He was discharged five days post-injury with no residual deficits except two small, well-healed cheek scars.

Lesson learned, indeed!

Perhaps the most significant lesson I learned was to respect the hospital hierarchy. The County culture was dependent on a rigid system, not unlike that in the military. Trainees ascended the graduated level of responsibility based on experience and presumed increasing competence, from intern to junior resident to senior resident to chief resident. Theoretically, there was always a more senior backup available all hours of the day and night, in-house or on long-range beeper, up to and including the attending on-call and ultimately the director of service. It was called the chain of command. CYA—cover your ass—was a wise acronym indeed, especially since surgeons were occasionally SSW—sure, swift, and wrong.

ROAD TRIP

Fortified with a bottle of Scotch for the six-hour drive (none for the driver), my chief resident, an oral surgery intern, and I departed the

County at two a.m. one Saturday to drive to a temporomandibular joint (TMJ) conference in Cape Cod. At eight a.m., we pulled into the parking lot of the Dunfey Hyannis Hotel and Conference Center and scurried to the lobby men's room to wash up, brush our teeth, and change shirts. Just then, the keynote speaker walked into the restroom. Seeing our disheveled appearance, he inquired which OMS residency program we represented. Sheepishly, we blurted, "Kings County Hospital."

The renowned TMJ expert was one of the first on the OMS lecture circuit to espouse the internal derangement concept of TMJ disorders. The articular disc or meniscus is found to be anteriorly displaced, causing clicking, popping, pain, and limited jaw opening. The treatment becomes surgical if all conservative modalities, such as nonsteroidals, muscle relaxants, splint therapy, and physical therapy, fail. Disc plication is the answer. Excise a wedge of the attachment, and reposition the disc posteriorly. This was before the advent of TMJ arthroscopy.

At lunch, we went around the table spouting our TMJ experience. One particularly aggressive young surgeon from West Virginia chimed in that he had personally performed 200 plications in the past year. I couldn't imagine that 200 patients in West Virginia could have a TMJ disorder. My experience at these meetings indicated that you could take the statistics cited by these so-called specialists and divide them by a factor of ten.

After a brief afternoon session in the heated indoor pool and sauna, we settled in for a much-needed nap. We woke in time for the cocktail party in the lobby, followed by a seafood dinner at the Asa Bearse House, a short walk down Main Street. Afterward, we stumbled back to the hotel bar for a nightcap.

During several rounds of Jameson Irish Whiskey, we met an attractive young lady who lived on the Cape. When the bar closed at two a.m., she invited the three of us back to her house. As clothes started flying off, she asked if one of us had a camera and could take some photos of her. One of us retrieved a small old-fashioned SLR camera from the car. He returned with the camera and started to snap photos of her discreetly, to avoid capturing any of us in the pictures. When it was my turn, sure enough we ran out of film. "No problem," my colleague whispered. "She doesn't know that. Keep shooting." Problem solved.

Twenty plus years later, I applied for the chairman position at the University of Florida at Gainesville. I flew into Atlanta from Newark airport, then took a puddle jumper to Gainesville for my interview. It was the aforementioned keynote speaker, now head of the search committee, who came to pick me up at the airport.

I recounted our first meeting at the Dunfey Hyannis. Did he remember? A wry grin settled on his face. The two-day interview process was both cordial and professional. Unfortunately, as an MD, DDS dual-degree candidate, I lost out to an outstanding MD, PhD, DDS triple-degree surgeon.

Small world indeed.

OUTING

My junior resident year culminated in June 1981, with our annual outing at the chairman's country club in Westchester. In the morning, former residents, many of whom had gone on to advanced subspecialty fellowship training, would present lectures. Lunch would be followed by golf or tennis, a cocktail party, and formal dinner. At dinner, the program directors of the various residency programs at the County would lavish praise on their graduating residents. Once I became program director, I would recount the surgical and academic accomplishments of the year before roasting the chief residents.

During my junior resident year, one of my CRs took no guff from the patients (including inmates from the prison ward) or from her male co-residents. One afternoon during teatime in the residents' room, she blurted, to my intern colleague's utter dismay, that she was *not* responsible for his education. This was, of course, contrary to the Socratic method of resident training.

While the chairman was busy giving his annual "Banner Year" speech, claiming credit for yet another outstanding year, this chief resident imbibed far too many cocktails. She stood up, then vomited under the table in the fancy dining room. Seemingly unfazed, she sat back down as if nothing had happened. Nonplussed, the seven other residents got up and switched to the last open table. After dessert, we carried the CR out of the club, and one of the dental interns had the ignominious task of driving her home in her own car.

Another thirty years would pass before we would graduate another female OMS resident. In the subsequent ten years as PD, I would accept eight female residents into the program.

Chief Resident Year

I LOOKED FORWARD to finally operating on major OR cases. With pent up excitement, I began my chief resident year on July 1, 1981. There would be major trauma cases, pathology and reconstructive surgery, orthognathic-corrective jaw surgery for skeletofacial defects, TMJ cases, interventions for major life-threatening cervicofacial infections, and a smattering of cosmetic procedures.

In terms of patient management, case selection, and resident logistics, the program was essentially resident run. In those early days, our dental department chairman kept mostly to his faculty practice at Downstate. We were fortunate to have Dr. Gold as our outstanding, albeit half-time, OMS PD. His pearls of wisdom regarding routine office oral surgery and general anesthesia would be lodged in the back of my mind for my forty years of practice. The exception occurred during lunchtime every Thursday, when both the PD and chairman would join us for grand rounds to review the previous week's OR cases, discuss the upcoming scheduled cases, and pimp the interns and junior residents. The chief residents were on the hot seat at the morbidity and mortality (M&M) conference, presenting complications and misadventures from the previous week. But when it came to the expanding scope of maxillofacial surgery, this was most often resident driven.

Early in my chief year, I found myself in the hospital on a lovely fall Sunday afternoon doing last-minute model surgery in preparation for an orthognathic case scheduled for the very next day. While I was busy in our clinic lab, the junior resident on-call was paged stat to the acute trauma area. He returned, looking incredulous, to summon me to join him. Although I still had hours of lab work to complete before

I could get the case to the OR table the next day, I begrudgingly complied. In the C-1 trauma bay, I saw EMS frantically attempting to maneuver a young boy, impaled on a black wrought-iron fence, from the ambulance to the ER gurney. The spiked top of the solid iron fence had pierced the submental region under his chin, traversed the floor of his mouth and anterior tongue, avulsed his maxillary central incisors, and exited his mouth splitting his upper lip.

According to his hysterical mother, this healthy eight-year-old had been rollerskating with his friend in the park, where he attempted to scale a five-foot-high fence; apparently, he'd been unsuccessful. EMS feared a severe vascular injury if they attempted to lift him off the fence in the field. Instead, they cut the fence using the Jaws of Life and transported him still impaled on a spiked five-by-five section of wrought iron. Pediatric surgery and anesthesia were also paged stat; the pediatric surgery attending was already in the house.

Although the patient was remarkably calm, all services agreed to take him emergently to the OR. There, in a more controlled setting, we could extricate him from the fence, intubate him or trach him to secure his airway, and control any significant bleeding. His penetrating entrance and exit wounds seemed anterior and midline enough to mitigate against major vascular injury.

We carefully shifted the boy from the stretcher to the OR table. Two large bore IVs and monitors were placed. The anesthesia attending slowly induced general anesthesia, hoping the patient wouldn't buck on the iron spike or vomit with an unsecured airway. Once the patient was asleep, my junior resident and I extricated the spiked fence inferiorly while anesthesia stabilized the head and neck. Then, anesthesia expeditiously intubated the patient. We encountered no major bleeding. We sutured the oral mucosa and tongue, then packed the skin entrance wound and tract. This rather lucky young lad was taken, still intubated as an airway precaution, to the pediatric SICU. He was extubated uneventfully the next morning and discharged home to the care of his grateful mother.

Although I had to stay late to finish the model surgery after the OR on Sunday, the orthognathic case went off as planned on Monday.

~

During my CR year, my co-resident and I were often at odds with our mostly bread-and-butter basic oral surgery trained OR attendings. We were fortunate enough that our program director brought his young partner on board as our go-to-guy for difficult cases in the OR.

One Sunday afternoon, this attending and I took a NYC cop emergently to the OR for a GSW to the anterior jaw. No significant vascular injury was discerned; angiography wasn't indicated. We performed the first tracheostomy in the history of the OMS department to secure the patient's airway due to his anticipated floor-of-mouth swelling. We then proceeded to debride and perform a closed reduction of his comminuted mandible fracture.

Upon returning the patient to the SICU post-op, I introduced the attending to a lovely nurse taking care of the patient; she would become his wife.

~

In 1981, we were still in the incipient stage delving into facial cosmetic surgery. My first such patient was a lovely, healthy, middle-aged Black woman who presented with a redundant, everted, prominent lower lip, for which she sought correction. A reduction cheiloplasty was indicated and agreed upon with my PD at grand rounds the day before the scheduled surgery. It should have been a chip shot and an opportunity to "suck at the teat of knowledge" as the OR attending would often say.

The OR attending was not present at rounds to discuss the case. The chairman was on vacation. That did not stop him from vociferously voicing his displeasure with the treatment plan in the OR holding area. I pressed on with the support of my PD, whom I reached pre-operatively via telephone. The OR attending was livid, especially since it was now two p.m. and the third case of the day. This particular attending was notorious for having to beat the Friday afternoon traffic out to Montauk, Long Island. I assured him we would be out of the OR by four p.m. We proceeded to start the case under IV sedation and local anesthesia.

The plan? To perform a wedge elliptical incision of redundant granulomatous mucosa and submucosa from commissure to commissure (corners of the mouth). The key to the procedure was to stay superficial to the orbicularis muscle of the lower lip. However, I didn't anticipate the prominence of the muscle itself, which required reduction to afford a cosmetic closure without tension. During this reduction process, I encountered multiple bleeders of the highly vascular lip, which required meticulous cauterization before closure. I finally accomplished this with the now furious attending screaming in my ear the entire case. Ultimately, we got the patient off the table and the attending out to Montauk by four p.m. to walk his dogs.

I called him later that night to apologize for forcing the case somewhat unexpectedly upon him. We agreed that attending presence at grand rounds should be mandatory. This would continue to be an issue that I would encounter with my entire attending staff for the next thirty-seven years.

After multiple cocktails that evening to calm my nerves, I woke up at six a.m. to head into Brooklyn for Saturday early-morning rounds with the program director. He had a habit of coming to morning rounds to see the post-operative patients at seven a.m. on the way to his office on Pitkin Avenue. In the B building elevator, he told me the OR attending had contacted him the prior night and was still furious. I assured the PD that I had called him, and it was all water under the bridge.

The intern who had prerounded earlier that morning assured us that our patient was stable, hemostatic, and ready for discharge. Then we walked into the patient's six-bed room and pulled back her curtain. Her lower lip was the size of a sausage! With the addition of a long-acting steroid, some TLC, and her good-natured attitude, her edema resolved slowly over the next two weeks. Fortunately for the patient and me, she ended up with a fine result.

~

By the spring of my chief resident year, I was starting to feel more self-confident as a surgeon and self-assured running the service. Inevitably, this caused more conflicts with the chairman, who threatened to fire me on a seemingly monthly basis for various degrees of insubordination. Then, one afternoon in March, he did it. This was before the concept of union-negotiated due process and the need for an administrative paper trail. In 1982, you could get axed three months before the residency finish line without recourse.

Of course, I had committed the cardinal sin. It was a busy Thursday afternoon clinic, and my co-chief was on vacation for the week. That left me alone to do the general anesthesia cases, run the service, conduct grand rounds, and pre-op the two cases for the Friday OR. Then, I was summoned by the chairman's office manager, ostensibly to drop everything and run across the street to his Downstate private office. There, one of his crony's kids was in from college during spring break for extraction of his four impacted wisdom teeth. The office had no general anesthesia capability, outdated instrumentation, and a nonsurgical assistant; this was a prescription for disaster that would take me an hour. So, I blew her off. I told her I would try to get there as soon as possible. An hour later, the office manager, now furious, called me back demanding I come right over. Instead, I sent her an intern to start the case, knowing full well he could never complete the procedure. On cue, she called back demanding my presence immediately, or she was going to call the chairman, who was busy in a Downstate medical board meeting. Defiantly, I reminded her that I didn't work for nor answer to her. That was the final straw.

Nary five minutes later, the now red-faced chairman, having sprinted across Clarkson Avenue to our Kings County clinic, stormed into the GA room and yelled, "You're fired." This was long before Donald Trump and *The Apprentice*, so I didn't quite appreciate the entertainment value. I was speechless; there was no sense in disputing my level of insubordination. I retrieved my backpack and left the premises.

I had barely driven back over the Brooklyn Bridge into Manhattan toward my apartment in Stuyvesant Town on 14th Street when I got a call from my exasperated program director. He had similarly just been summoned across the street to the still apoplectic chairman's Downstate office. He reminded the chairman that he couldn't fire me, at least not today. We had a departmental monthly meeting that night, and I was the sole scheduled speaker. I turned around and drove back over the Brooklyn Bridge into Brooklyn.

After that near-firing episode so close to the finish line, I decided to behave myself until residency graduation on June 30, 1982, and check the remaining boxes. There was an oral presentation to give at the New York Institute of Clinical Oral Pathology (NYICOP) and a paper to write that would be suitable for publication in a peer-reviewed journal.

Mostly, I focused on job hunting. In those days, there were not many OMS associate positions available—certainly not the plethora of opportunities available to current grads starting at $250,000 per year. Wanting to stay in the Greater New York area, I interviewed with the usual three practices that had a well-known revolving door of associates. They all paid peanuts at $30,000 per year plus meager benefits. That was frankly embarrassing after spending eight years at Columbia and completing three years of residency, with student loans still left to pay off.

Workplace Security

KINGS COUNTY HOSPITAL in the 1980s wasn't the safest work environment. Back in October 1982, a thirty-three-year-old previously convicted burglar seized five hostages at the hospital. He held a large contingent of both hospital and NYC police at bay for forty-six hours. He eventually released the hostages and was peacefully taken into custody.

Three years later, a disgruntled forty-seven-year-old former thoracic surgery patient at the County concealed a sawed-off shotgun in a blue canvas shoulder bag and walked into the hospital. He took the elevator up to the fourth-floor office of Dr. Thomas Pollack, a forty-year-old general surgery attending and director of surgical service at the County. I had come to know Dr. Pollack during my previous SICU rotation when he covered the unit that month. A great guy, he took the time to talk to a mere oral surgery rotator like me. I learned that he had trained at New York Hospital-Cornell and was married with three young children.

The patient—seeing Dr. Pollack through his open office door, sitting with his back turned—shot Dr. Pollack in the side of his chest. He calmly walked away from the scene, down the staircase, exiting the hospital. Days later, police apprehended him. An hour later, Dr. Pollack died on the operating table, ironically in the very hospital he served.

Turns out it was a case of mistaken identity. Dr. Pollack wasn't even the surgeon who had operated on the man earlier in the year. The shooter never saw his face. I attended Dr. Pollack's memorial service at the hospital.

In subsequent years, security was beefed up at the County. I always found the hospital police readily available and effective. Perhaps it was foolhardy on my part, but I always felt a false sense of security walking around Clarkson Avenue in my long white coat. New York City police were always responsive.

Unfortunately, that didn't preclude the occasional robbery. One OMS intern opted to avoid paying the monthly garage fee by parking on the street. A costly mistake. At lunchtime, this intern went to retrieve something from his car. As he approached, he was surprised to see a man ransacking his car. Startled, the thief ran off with the car radio. The intern couldn't catch him, but he got a good look at him and reported the incident to hospital police.

The next morning, this intern was busy in the Oral Surgery Clinic. He walked into one of the treatment rooms, and much to his surprise, the very same thief was sitting in the dental chair complaining of a toothache. The intern calmly exited the room and called security. Hospital police detained the accused suspect until two New York City cops arrived to arrest him. The intern had to go to the 71st Precinct on nearby Empire Boulevard to file a formal complaint. To make matters worse, the suspect was released with a summons to appear in court before the intern could even finish the paperwork.

~

Eventually, I took a full-time job at a so-called group practice in beautiful downtown Newark, New Jersey—four-and-a-half days per week for $40,000 plus my malpractice insurance. The Who's Who of Newark notables includes Aaron Burr, the aforementioned Ed Koch, Jerry Lewis, Frankie Valli, Shaquille O'Neal, Queen Latifah, and Whitney Houston. The practice served an upscale predominantly Black clientele that included local professional athletes and entertainers. I had Mondays off, so I volunteered at Kings County as an OR attending to get my required major cases for my specialty boards.

It was a reasonably safe practice by Newark standards, where the projects were almost burnt to the ground in the riots of 1967. Safe for me, that is, until one February day in 1983 when a blizzard hit

Newark earlier in the day than forecast. I stopped patient registration by one p.m. in hopes of leaving by three p.m. before the roads would become impassable. I was living in a condo in Fort Lee, New Jersey, by the George Washington Bridge, which was usually a thirty-minute commute. By three p.m., it was already snowing heavily. Just as I was closing up shop, one of the general dentists downstairs referred an emergency patient to oral surgery. The patient, an eighteen-year-old healthy Black woman, had a pericoronitis or infection associated with an impacted wisdom tooth. It would have taken at least half an hour to complete the procedure and wake up the patient, who demanded general anesthesia. So, instead, I wrote her temporizing prescriptions for antibiotics and narcotic pain meds, and I advised her to seek treatment at the University Hospital ER if her symptoms worsened.

I was about to leave when I heard a commotion in the waiting room. The patient's boyfriend was brandishing a gun at my receptionist and demanding that I treat his girlfriend. The receptionist had hit the panic button, but it would be ten minutes before the police arrived with the rapidly accumulating snow. Unfortunately, our security guard had just left, assuming we were done for the day. Now, my experience at the Kings County Knife and Gun Club indicated that it was a .22-caliber pistol. I tried to calm the patient's boyfriend and persuade him to lower his weapon, to no avail.

Terrified, I agreed to treat his girlfriend. The receptionist had no choice but to stay and assist me. The procedure went well without any complications. The police arrived and secured the weapon. They chose not to arrest the boyfriend. It was now almost four p.m. and getting dark when we all exited the building, with a police escort, to the parking lot. Eight inches of fresh snow had already fallen. Over the poorly plowed streets, my new Toyota Celica GT, with its manual stick shift, was too low to the ground to safely navigate the accumulating snow and ice. I drove as far as Newark Penn Station, then had to give up. I ditched the car in an unplowed parking lot. When I exited the car, I noticed a flat rear tire on the driver's side. I wondered, was this a coincidence or a thank you from the gun-toting boyfriend?

I boarded the last New Jersey Transit train still running to New York Penn Station. Once in Manhattan, I hopped on the #1 uptown express subway to 72nd Street. The liquor store at the corner of Amsterdam Avenue and 70th Street was still open. I took my newly purchased fifth of Remy Martin VSOP cognac into 1 Nevada Tower. The doorman buzzed the intercom upstairs as I took the elevator to the twelfth floor. My mother greeted me at the door to her apartment. After several cognacs to warm me up and calm her down, we agreed that Newark wasn't my long-term career solution.

Private Practice

THE NEXT TWO YEARS were eventful. I had three major exams to study for as I put my private practice plans on hold. Buying a practice or starting one from scratch would have to wait for a while. In 1983, I passed my American Association of Oral and Maxillofacial Surgeons and American Dental Society of Anesthesiology fellowship exams. When one of my former OR attendings stepped down, I landed a paid Friday OR slot at the County.

During my resident days as I grew more confident as a surgeon, I also gained self-confidence socially. This paid dividends with externs and nurses. One Friday night in 1980, I had visited a popular Upper East Side establishment, the Sugar Mill, for drinks with two of my co-residents. I was hanging out at the bar with one of my colleagues when an attractive young lady approached us. Truth be told, she seemed more interested in my friend than me. However, after a while, he blew us off, leaving just the two of us talking over cocktails for the better part of an hour. Since I was on-call the next day, I excused myself and left.

When I reached my car, it occurred to me that I had not asked for her phone number. *Too late now*, I thought as I started the car to drive home. After making a quick left onto East End Avenue, midway into the intersection, I noticed a car with four women stopped at the light. The young lady from the bar—Helaine—rolled down her window and gave me her phone number. Coincidence, fate, or did she mastermind the whole encounter? Two weeks later, while post-call from the trauma surgery service, I woke up at eight p.m. Even though it was late, I thought what the hell and gave her a call to see if she wanted to go to dinner. I'm sure she had already eaten, but she accompanied me anyway.

We started dating. I also learned the hard way to never treat friends or family. It's bound to be a Murphy's Law disaster. In 1982, during my chief resident year, I extracted Helaine's wisdom teeth. The surgery was routine. On the way to her apartment on Roosevelt Island, we picked up the prescriptions for amoxicillin and Percocet (oxycodone plus acetaminophen) I had called in to her strip mall pharmacy. That's when I had the brainstorm to stop for Chinese take-out, thinking wonton soup would be the perfect elixir for her. When I returned to the car, tears were running down her cheeks. The local anesthesia had evidently worn off. I learned my lesson the hard way: Always give a long-acting anesthetic for the road. To this day, she has never forgiven me.

The rest is history.

Upon completion of my residency, Helaine and I moved into a condo in Fort Lee for a couple of years before we tied the knot. In June 1984, at thirty-one years old, I finally decided to settle down and get married.

My next big milestone? After studying for the obligatory six months and taking the prerequisite LSU review course, I was finally ready to take my specialty boards. In February 1985, I flew to Chicago in a snowstorm and took a cab to the old Drake Hotel, the site of the exam. After a dinner of Chicago deep-dish pizza, I was as ready as I was going to get. My exam started the next day at eight a.m. and ended at noon. It went by in a blur. By one p.m., I was back in the cab to O'Hare airport with no clue whether I had passed the test. Five weeks later, I received the thin blue envelope signifying that I was now a Diplomate of the American Board of Oral and Maxillofacial Surgery. (Twenty years later, I finally became a Board Examiner in Dallas, the new exam site at the time).

Having checked off all the personal and professional boxes, it was now time to open my own practice. Fortunately, during my three long associate years in Newark, I had also joined the OMS staff at Newark Beth Israel Medical Center (NBIMC). It was and remains the heart transplant center for New Jersey. Once I passed my boards, I petitioned the medical board to obtain privileges to perform histories and physicals on my own inpatients. I was the first OMS granted such privileges at NBIMC. There, I met Dr. R. David Seldin, my future partner and lifelong friend. To this day, I have never heard anyone utter a bad word about him. He had a long-established, well-respected OMS practice in the Robert Treat Hotel in beautiful downtown Newark. Built in 1916, President Woodrow Wilson was one of its first guests.

We formed a partnership. I would purchase a half share in the Newark practice, and we would open a satellite office in Teaneck. Teaneck made a lot of sense to both of us. It was where Dave had grown up, and I was planning to buy a house there. We scouted out office space on Cedar Lane and began construction on our new office in the winter of 1985. We opened the day after the Super Bowl, February 1986.

In this new setting, I quickly confirmed that I was still not suited for OMS private practice. Dealing with referring general dentists did not turn out to be my strong suit. I also had no patience for the local community hospital politics and inter-specialty turf wars. No one ever accused me of being tactful. A couple of examples will serve to highlight that.

Dave Seldin and I slowly, but surely, built up our Teaneck referral base. This required boring lunches and dinners on the rubber chicken circuit with local general dentists, periodontists, pedodontists, ortho-dontists, and prosthodontists. Surprisingly, one such dentist on Cedar Lane, in the center of town, became my own treating dentist and lifelong friend.

But the rest of them proved the adage that referring dentists are only as good as their last referral. Case in point was the main prosthodontist in town, who happened to have been an instructor of mine at Columbia School of Dental and Oral Surgery. He was a contemporary of my partner, who took it upon himself to culti-vate the relationship. Dave was an "A" flight tennis player while the referring guy was a "C" player who loved the sport. So, my partner sucked it up and signed up to play with him weekly at the local indoor tennis bubble for what seemed to be an exorbitant fee. We considered it a business expense.

Every Monday night after work, my partner trudged off to play. He had no anticipation of even breaking a sweat. All winter and spring they played on. That is, until one day I stopped at the prosthodontist's office to drop off some referral cards. While I was chatting with the receptionist, out of the corner of my eye I happened to see one of our OMS competitors from the adjoining town. He was hard at work extracting impacted wisdom teeth on this supposed trustworthy referring dentist's patient.

The next day I ran into this competitor at a local hospital meeting. "You fucking whore," I blurted while he sheepishly avoided my stare. "How dare you come into my town and prostitute yourself out?" I yelled. Needless to say, my partner never played another set with that prosthodontist again. Like I said, a referring dentist is only as good as his last referral.

The local hospital was directly across the street from our office and only five minutes from my new house. It was a great setup for me geographically except for the bullshit. Community hospital politics were equally problematic for me from both an intra- and inter-departmental perspective. Both sets of battles were often economically based.

At one well-attended dental meeting (yes, we were only a dental division in the Department of Surgery), I proceeded to get into a heated argument with the division chief. He was a competing OMS from two towns away who considered himself a TMJ expert. He attempted to protect his TMJ turf for personal financial gain by limiting all other surgeons' TMJ arthroscopy privileges. I stood up and challenged him based on my arthroscopic experience as an OR attending at Kings County. I probably should have stopped there, as the other dentists in the room already seemed to be on my side. But that wasn't my style. I stated that he had no right to limit my privileges since I happened to be board certified and he wasn't. Again, I never said I was tactful.

Reluctantly, he did sign off on my TMJ privileges.

Inter-departmental turf wars were particularly disconcerting to me. The facial trauma coverage protocol was based solely on economics. OMS covered all the mandible fractures and oral trauma, much of which occurred in uninsured, assaulted patients. Plastics and ENT split the midface trauma, which typically occurred in motor vehicle accident patients covered by New Jersey no-fault insurance—unless, of course, the patient was uninsured. If so, the OMS service was somehow miraculously consulted. As an active attending at a busy Level I trauma center in Brooklyn, I found this arrangement degrading.

Nonetheless, I continued to take OMS trauma calls at the local hospital to build up our practice. I did so until two a.m. New Year's Day 1989, when I was paged to the ER at Holy Name Medical Center for a facial trauma. The patient was a young female driver who had struck her face on the steering wheel post motor vehicle accident. I arrived within ten minutes to find the patient awake, alert, and in a cervical collar until C-spine fracture could be ruled out. She had sustained a maxillary alveolar fracture (the segment of bone housing the upper anterior teeth) and a lengthy through-and-through upper lip laceration. Evidently, the on-call plastic surgeon had been consulted first and had performed a beautiful plastic layered closure of the lip lac. Unfortunately, he failed to follow the basic tenet of facial trauma, which is to deal with the teeth and bone first before the soft tissue. I advised the patient and ER MD that to reduce and stabilize her alveolar fracture and multiple partially avulsed mobile teeth, I would have to wire an arch bar splint in place. Undoubtedly, her lip would split wide open again. Sure enough, I re-sutured the lip at the completion of the procedure.

The next day, I contacted the plastic surgeon and emergency medicine doctor to thank them for their "timely" consultation. And, by the way, I removed my name from the OMS on-call schedule. For my New Year's resolution, I vowed never to be a second-class citizen in any hospital again.

~

While Dave and I sought to expand our new Teaneck office while still maintaining our busy Newark practice, I continued as a Friday OR OMS attending at the County. As the youngest and most aggressive OR attending, often I supervised the most complex cases as the residents pushed to expand the scope of maxillofacial surgery. I wanted to pursue dual-degree training to support this expanded scope.

It was time to go back to medical school.

In the late 1980s, dual-degree MD/OMS residency programs were popping up across the country. Starting with Massachusetts General and the University of Alabama, by 1989 more than twenty dual-degree programs out of the 108 OMS residency programs in the country offered an integrated six-year MD/OMS track. By 2019, that number would plateau at forty-six dual-degree programs out of 101 residency programs.

My chairman and I had several feasibility discussions on the subject. I had expressed to him a sincere interest to attend medical school with the intention of returning as the OMS residency program director of a new integrated dual-degree program. Surprisingly, he was supportive of the idea. More importantly, he had connections at Downstate Medical College, SUNY Brooklyn. The dean of the medical school and several department chairmen had been his patients over the years. He arranged an interview for me with the dean. I was now on my own.

The dean was an impressive yet stern figure. As chairman of OB-GYN as well as dean of the medical school, he would go on to serve as provost and subsequently president of SUNY Downstate. He was a no-nonsense sort. He asked me only one question: "Why do you want to go back to medical school at this point in your established career?" I explained that with the newly expanded scope of contemporary maxillofacial surgery, a medical background was necessary to better medically manage and surgically treat these patients.

He carefully perused my curriculum vitae and transcripts, noting that I had attended Columbia for eight years. I explained that Columbia School of Dental and Oral Surgery was, in fact, a co-curriculum school. That meant that I had taken my first two years of basic sciences with the Columbia College of Physicians and Surgeons medical students. He put down his glasses and carefully offered up a proposal. He would grant me advanced standing into the third-year medical school class beginning that July 1 on one condition: I had to pass the National Board of Medical Examiners (NBME) Step 1 exam (now the United States Medical Licensing Examination or USMLE Step 1). I would be granted only one attempt. I gratefully thanked him and shook his hand on my way out of his office.

Once back in my car, it finally hit me. The good news: I was just offered admission with advanced standing to a fully accredited US medical school. The bad news: I had only five months to study for the most difficult exam of my life that would focus on the very basic sciences that I had last studied twelve years ago. It included biochemistry, anatomy, physiology, pathology, microbiology, histology, pharmacology, neuroscience, statistics, and epidemiology. While studying, I had to work at two offices six days per week. And by the way, my wife was due with our first child in May.

Dave was shocked and taken aback to hear of my decision. It truly hurt to tell him that I would have to leave the practice, as medical school was a full-time proposition. Being the great friend that he was, he grew supportive of my decision. We amicably agreed, with minimal attorney interference, on a buyout that provided me with the income to live on while in medical school. However, he had to swiftly proceed to find another partner or associate to replace me. That left me no fallback position if I failed the exam.

My wife was equally supportive as she recognized this was something I had a visceral need to pursue, with one caveat that is. I had to promise to only complete the two years of medical school and one year of general surgery required for medical licensure. I would not pursue additional residency training in another specialty. I agreed.

The next five months were an ordeal as I sought to balance work and studying. The exam was rigorous with a 16 percent failure rate. In those days, study aids such as *First Aid, World,* or *Pathoma* did not exist. I studied at home after work every weeknight. I spent a half day on Saturdays and all-day Sundays at the Kaplan prep center in Hackensack taking old practice exams. At the Kaplan center, I was surrounded by foreign medical students desperately seeking to pass the Federation Licensing Exam (FLEX), which served as a pathway into an accredited US medical school.

Anticipating a major lifestyle change, I scheduled my Step 1 in early May before my wife was due. It was a day and a half of absolute torture, with eight hours on day one followed by four hours on day two. One hour into the exam, a throbbing headache began, and it plagued me for the rest of the day. I left after the second day having no confidence that I had passed the test.

Our first daughter, Margot, was born two weeks later, on Mother's Day. She would grow up to become a pediatric neuro-oncologist at Nationwide Children's Hospital in Columbus, Ohio, thirty-three years later.

One month after taking the exam, I received a letter from the NBME. I slowly opened it: "PASS." On to medical school!

Medical School

I STARTED MEDICAL SCHOOL as a third-year student (MS III) in July 1989. At thirty-six, I was twelve years older and more experienced than my medical school classmates. Most of my medical school attendings were suspicious as to my intentions. Some assumed I aimed to simply better perform fillings and cleanings on an older and sicker patient population. *Really?* I continued to function one Friday per month as an OMS OR attending to earn some money and maintain my surgical skills.

I began my first clerkships—rotations to all the different medical specialties—in mid-July, on the psychiatry service at Methodist Hospital. Methodist is in the middle of Park Slope, Brooklyn; the "Slope" was in its nascent gentrification phase, with outstanding bars and restaurants. Al Capone's townhouse on Garfield Place was priced at $2.5 million in 2017.

Psychiatry at Methodist was renowned for its electroconvulsive therapy (ECT) unit. Performed under ambulatory general anesthesia, a targeted electric current is passed through the brain that triggers a brief seizure. The seizure causes release of neurotransmitters to reverse severe depression and suicidal ideation refractory to antidepressants. Not without its side effects, ECT can cause recent retrograde amnesia. This version of ECT was infinitely safer than in the early "electric shock therapy" days of the 1940s.

ECT is typically performed three times weekly. Inpatients and outpatients would line up outside the ECT unit every Monday, Wednesday, and Friday morning. Often catatonic with a slow shuffling gait and unkempt in appearance, they would enter the operating suite. After ECT and brief recovery from the short-acting general anesthetic and muscle relaxant, they would exit rejuvenated and energized with their batteries recharged. ECT was remarkably quick and effective, albeit temporary in nature, so patients still had to resume their meds.

Every Friday night for six weeks, I returned to Kings County for my weekly psych emergency room rotation. The G building emergency room was the acute intake psychiatric facility for Brooklyn, serving as the equivalent to what Bellevue was to Manhattan. The infamous G building had housed serial killer David Berkowitz, aka Son of Sam, after his arrest on August 10, 1977. Ultimately, Berkowitz pleaded guilty to eight separate shooting attacks and six murders in New York City from the summer of 1976 to July 1977. He claimed to have obeyed the orders of the demonic dog Harvey, who belonged to his neighbor Sam Carr.

Friday nights were particularly wild, with a steady stream of potentially violent psychotic patients admitted to the holding area. As a third-year medical student rotator, I had to interview one new patient each night. I was to perform a mental status exam and psychiatric assessment and submit my write-up to the second-year psych resident on-call. On my very first Friday night slot, I quickly learned Lesson #1: Always have a cop nearby. As I started to interview a seemingly well sedated, supposedly nonviolent middle-aged male with a documented history of schizophrenia, he lunged across the table at me. One of New York City's finest jumped in to defuse the situation before I would have ended up in the main hospital ER.

Of course, I was assigned my share of schizophrenic and bipolar inpatients to follow at Methodist. My favorite was a middle-aged, manic depressive White male. When he was in his manic phase, he was wired. He could go days without sleeping while remaining totally euphoric. At the nurse's station, he would demand to be released so he could take the train to Washington, DC. He needed to meet with President George H. W. Bush, then fly to Moscow to talk to soon-to-be Russian President Mikhail Gorbachev, then take a boat to see British Prime Minister Margaret Thatcher. Only he was able to solve all international diplomatic conflicts. It was a major challenge to control his lithium dosage, with its narrow therapeutic window.

Each of the major three-month clerkships (medicine, pediatrics, and surgery) required passing a rigorous written shelf test and oral examination after rotating through each medical specialty. The six-week neurology clerkship, in the era before the seemingly mandatory CT scan or MRI, required some diagnostic acumen with use of the reflex hammer and tuning fork all medical students were required to carry. Lastly, obstetrics and gynecology was the most rigorous clerkship, with subspecialty mini-rotations on obstetrics, gynecology, gyn oncology, and gyn endocrine all in a six-week period. OB-GYN certainly afforded me my most memorable third-year patient encounters.

One day, I was assigned to join the gyn team in the B building main OR room #3. As the third-year medical student, I had to assist the gyn chief resident and attending, who were performing a transvaginal hysterectomy for fibroids. Usually done via an open abdominal incision, the transvaginal approach was an acceptable but technically more difficult approach for benign disease of the uterus. OR #3 was only two doors down from OR #1, which was the OMS operating suite on Mondays and Fridays for my past ten years. I quickly scrubbed and entered OR #3.

The scrub nurse, a longtime friend, gowned and gloved me. She whispered in my ear, "What the hell are you doing here? This isn't your part of the body!" The attending and CR were too preoccupied with their surgery to have overheard her and had no idea of my background. I made it a point of not volunteering it unless asked.

The dissection was tedious and quite vascular. Finally, they were about to deliver the uterus when all hell broke loose. They must have nicked a branch off the uterine artery, causing a major bleed. They both yelled at me to retract and put pressure on the wound. The anesthesiologist called urgently for two units of packed cells. The still-attached uterus obscured the surgeons' exposure from below. However, from my assistant's perch slightly cephalad (above), I could see the bleeder. The scrub nurse quietly handed me a curved hemostat. Reflexively, I clamped the vessel; the bleeding stopped instantly. The attending and resident initially sighed, then placed two hemoclips proximally and distally to ligate the vessel.

Simultaneously, it occurred to them that a mere third-year medical student had gained control of the vessel. "Where the hell did you learn that maneuver?" they asked incredulously. "I saw it on TV," I replied, attempting to add some levity. The scrub nurse then informed them that I wasn't a typical medical student, but rather an OMS OR attending. The surgeons completed the operation in silence, and the patient was transferred to the recovery room in stable condition. News of my intervention spread throughout the OB-GYN service. Initially, I was reprimanded but ultimately praised by most of my peers.

~

The Friday afternoon gyn clinic, especially before a golden weekend off-call, could be absolute torture. One warm spring Friday was particularly memorable. The three MS IIIs on the service were assigned their own cubicle to examine clinic patients with various gynecological maladies. At four p.m., I was ready for my last patient of the session, a twenty-two-year-old moderately obese Black woman. Upon asking her what brought her to the clinic, she blurted a diatribe. "My boyfriend says it be stankin' down there. He fucked me but won't go down on me anymore."

While she helped the patient don a paper gown and get settled into the stirrups, the experienced nurse, with speculum and air freshener in hand, suggested I try a eucalyptus sucking candy under my mask. I tried to insert the vaginal speculum, but its passage was blocked. By now, my eyes were tearing and my nasal hairs were burning. I summoned the attending covering the clinic, who guided me as I cautiously passed the speculum around an apparent foreign body.

With a pair of tongs, I gently removed a foul-smelling greenish object. It was two tampons stuck together! The patient sheepishly admitted that she must have left them in place for at least two months.

~

After completing the third-year clerkships, the fourth year of medical school was easy. It was comprised of all electives except for six weeks of mandatory family practice. I conveniently arranged my family practice clerkship offsite at St. Mary's Hospital in Hoboken, New Jersey, an easy commute from my home in Teaneck. The "Mile Square City" is on the banks of the Hudson River across from lower Manhattan. It is famously the childhood home of Frank Sinatra. In the summer of 1990, it too was in its early gentrification phase, with up-and-coming bars and restaurants along Washington Avenue.

St. Mary's was a primary care community hospital; family practice was its only residency program. There, I sutured lacerations in the ER, examined patients with garden variety maladies, such as diabetes, hypertension, and COPD, wrote a plethora of prescriptions, and ordered referrals to specialists across the river.

Around Thanksgiving 1990, I won the lottery among fourth-year medical students to participate in the Lucy Frank Squire, MD radiology course at SUNY Downstate. Dr. Squire was the first woman enrolled in the Massachusetts General Hospital Radiology residency program in 1940. She won the initial Marie Curie Award from the American Association of Women Radiologists in 1987. Her landmark text, *Fundamentals of Radiology*, has been the gold standard in medical education for sixty years. The course was encyclopedic, with more than 2,000 radiographs to review in four weeks.

I thoroughly enjoyed my daily interaction with this icon of medical education until I notified her of my anticipated absence the following day. I explained that I planned to pick up my wife and newborn daughter from the hospital post C-section. Much to my chagrin, she gruffly advised me that my absence on the day of her practical review would make it highly unlikely that I would pass her final exam. I told her I would take my chances. Two days later, I aced that exam. By the way, thirty-three years later, my younger daughter, Stefanie, completed her seventh and final year of general surgery residency at Beth Israel Deaconess Medical Center, one of the Harvard programs.

~

Bypassing vacations, I consolidated my fourth-year requirements and completed medical school by the end of February 1991. Prior to this, my chairman and I had arranged a meeting with the medical school dean and the chairman of the surgery department. The surgery chairman ruled the entire general surgery department with an iron fist. A call from his secretary to his eighth-floor office atop University Hospital was met with great apprehension by his chief residents.

We discussed the initiation of a dual-degree MD/OMS residency program at Kings County- SUNY Downstate. I reiterated to the dean the need for medical education to better manage our sick, older patient population. Given the expanding scope of maxillofacial surgery, I told the surgery chairman that a year of general surgery residency training would be beneficial to manage our surgical patients as well as to learn general surgical operating principles. That general surgery year would place us on par with the other surgical specialties. A year of general surgery was also essential for medical licensure in New York.

Surprisingly, I was met with little resistance. The chairman was aware of my performance during the surgery clerkship and was more than happy to scut me out for a year on general surgery.

I had done my research into existing integrated dual-degree residency programs. We all agreed on a six-year track for incoming residents. However, I would only have the final general surgery year to complete since I had finished all my OMS training. The first year would be an intern year on the OMS service, including time to pass the physical diagnosis course at the medical school and Step I to gain advanced standing into the third-year medical school class. The next two years would be spent in the medical school at the third- and fourth-year medical student level, with the resident receiving an MD degree upon graduation. This would be followed by a year as a general surgery intern.

The resident would return to the OMS service for the final two years of training, first as a senior resident then as chief resident. Upon satisfactory passage of the USMLE Step 2 and 3, in addition to the general surgery year, the resident would be eligible for medical licensure in New York and any other state that only requires one ACGME (Accreditation Council for Graduate Medical Education) accredited medical or surgical post-graduate year for licensure.

It was arranged for me to start my general surgery year in April 1991. By forfeiting my four weeks of vacation, I would complete my general surgery year by February 29, 1992.

General Surgery

WELCOME TO GEN SURG

On April Fools' Day, I joined the gen surg/tumor service at Kings County. I would manage to survive eleven nonstop months relatively unscathed; at thirty-eight years old, this was no easy task.

Before starting the rigorous year, my wife and I took our two daughters to Florida for a couple of weeks of rest and as much relaxation as was possible with a toddler and an infant.

All told, I performed more than 200 OR cases: Breast lumpectomies, lipoma excisions, hernias, hemorrhoids, I&Ds, and amputations were typical intern cases. I placed numerous central lines (internal jugular and subclavian), Swan-Ganz catheters, arterial lines, chest tubes, nasogastric tubes, and bladder catheters as I rotated on nine surgical services at Kings County-Downstate and three affiliated hospitals.

New York State had adopted the Bell Commission's 405 regulations limiting the resident work schedule to no more than twenty-four consecutive hours, or eighty hours per week, in 1989, but it was not strictly enforced in gen surg in 1991-1992. Typically, I had to be on-call every third night without sleep and then work in-house the next day until six p.m. after evening rounds, for a thirty-six-hour shift.

Falling asleep on the median divider heading north on FDR Drive to the George Washington Bridge was scary but not uncommon. Often, I would call my wife to stay awake on the drive home.

As I've told my OMS residents, that gen surg year will make a man (or woman) out of you. Still, I asked for no quarter and received none.

The general surgery service fostered its own unique culture of paranoia from the chairman that trickled downward to the interns. In the early 1990s, the ACGME still tolerated a pressure-packed pyramid system. The Downstate gen surgery residency program, as was the case for most university-level top surgery programs, accepted more categorical residents into the intern- and second-year slots than they had fifth-year chief resident positions to graduate. The big cut happened between the second and third year. The residents who didn't make the cut were farmed out to the research lab for one to two years. It was even suggested to some poor residents that they continue their training in another surgical subspecialty, for example urology.

Ironically, those very same residents who didn't make the cut in gen surg are now earning infinitely higher incomes as urologists in our current procedure-driven, insurance-based medical model. Office-based or ambulatory surgicenter procedures, such as prostate biopsies and cystoscopies, followed by in-hospital robotic prostatectomies, are a goldmine. This is especially true considering that one out of six men will be diagnosed (or overdiagnosed) with prostate cancer.

Besides the stress of the pyramid factor from below, there was senior-level competition from above to match into highly prestigious post-residency fellowships. Cardiothoracic surgery was perched atop the surgical pyramid before interventional cardiology would eventually cut into its coronary bypass monopoly with angioplasty/stenting. Vascular surgery, transplant surgery, plastic surgery, pediatric surgery, oncologic surgery, trauma/critical care, and the rear admirals of colorectal surgery all had their own stressful fellowship match process.

For those preliminary gen surg interns, such as myself, who matched for only one to two years as part of their integrated specialty residency program, it wasn't as cutthroat. Still, the tension was pervasive. Every intern, whether categorical or preliminary, dreaded the call from the gen surg secretary at Downstate to schedule a meeting with the chair to discuss a "clean kill" when he or she had "nuked" a patient. No one wanted to be dubbed "007-licensed to kill."

Worse yet, the chief resident on service was saddled with the ignominious task of presenting that complication or unexpected death at the weekly M&M conference in front of the entire department. Since shit flows downhill, that CR was certain to make the poor intern's life a living hell for the entire week. Additional on-call shifts or forced sabbatical from the OR for that intern was expected.

~

My first exposure to so-called general surgical principles occurred in the B building OR #2, right next door to my old OMS OR #1. But for all practical purposes, it was light-years away.

I was assisting on an exploratory laparotomy, or open abdominal approach, for a colon cancer case. In the pre-laparoscopic days, we had to make a large vertical midline peri-umbilical incision for adequate exposure. After resection of the cancerous segment of colon with appropriate negative margins, and then performing reanastomosis, or reconnection of the bowel to hopefully avoid a colostomy, we had to close the long incision in layers. The attending and CR, satisfied with my prior surgical experience, scrubbed out and left me to close with a medical student. The CR returned in thirty minutes to find the wound fully closed with a dressing in place. The CR, a somewhat pedantic sort, was incredulous. "Did you use one-handed or two-handed square surgical ties to close the fascia?"

Before I could respond that I had indeed used one-handed ties, he grabbed a suture scissor and reopened the skin layer. He placed his index finger between two sutures in the fascia and proceeded to lift the patient off the table. The wound remained intact. Nevertheless, he took the scissors and reopened the entire length of the wound. "Now, close it with two-handed surgical ties," he ordered as he stormed back out of the OR. "That's a good use of surgical and anesthesia time," I uttered to the scrub nurse, a longtime friend of mine. The medical student looked aghast as I reassured him, "Welcome to gen surg."

~

In May, I was off to the neurosurgery (NSx) service at Kings County Hospital and University Hospital across the street. To my surprise, my request for NSx for my elective month was honored. I had already rotated on the service for a month during a fourth-year medical student elective. As the field of OMS was starting to expand into the upper third of the face, I welcomed the experience and expertise I could glean from my NSx colleagues. In maxillofacial trauma, frontal sinus fractures required a bicoronal flap. In maxillofacial reconstruction, calvaria grafts harvested from the nondominant parietal bone and temporalis flaps required hemicoronal exposure as well. Although I was well aware of the rigors of the service, I looked forward to it.

In the early 1990s, the Kings County-Downstate NSx residency was one of the top programs in the country. The NSx residency match for graduating medical students was the most competitive of all specialties. It would be another decade before political squabbling would cause the demise of their NSx residency program. Accordingly, their residents were outstanding in their own right; several went on to become icons in the field. It was an arduous path for them with at least seven years of training, including one to two years of research in the NSx chairman's research lab. Eight years was par for the course. By the time they graduated from the program, each chief resident had performed more than 2,000 OR cases. They were fearless.

In those days on the County side, it was a resident-run program with the CR running the service. The Downstate side was attending driven, with the senior resident or CR scrubbing in with the highly respected chairman on his private cases. For the most part, I gratefully stayed on the County side of Clarkson Avenue.

It was a physically demanding month. I was on-call every other night, or rarely every third night, with a third- or fourth-year medical student wannabe. On-call, I ran the service at the County side while the junior resident covered Downstate and both NSx ICUs. We would meet up in the ER for admissions and acute trauma cases. I typically covered an in-house census of more than thirty NSx patients with head trauma such as subdural hematomas, brain tumors, cerebrovascular accidents (CVAs) or strokes, arteriovenous malformations

(AVMs), and spinal injuries.

Sleeping on-call was out of the question. Inpatients in various stages of neurological impairment would constantly pull out their IVs and/or nasogastric feeding tubes (NGT). Quickly, I quickly learned the rule of three.

Once the minimally responsive patient—i.e., "the lights were on, but nobody was home"—removed his or her NGT or softer Dobbhoff feeding tube for a third time in a single twenty-four-hour on-call session, this necessitated the infamous "Kentucky Sling." The NGT was passed through one naris (nostril) and retrieved with a clamp in the nasopharynx. It was then removed out of the mouth and passed through the contralateral nares down into the stomach. Regardless of cognition level, any attempt by the patient to remove the NGT elicited immediate nasal septal pain and tearing, which was enough to thwart any further attempts at removal. It was certainly less traumatic than round-the-clock wrist restraints.

Then, there was the referred patient from one of the local community hospitals without neurosurgical coverage for CVA, subarachnoid hemorrhage, head trauma, etc. In the predigital CT era, they would fax an almost illegible copy of a head CT to the ER physician, who would unilaterally accept transfer to the County before I could put the kibosh on it. My junior resident and I would meet in the ER to admit an essentially brain-dead patient to the service. Sure enough, by six a.m. rounds, the patient was invariably lying in the bed immediately adjacent to the NSx resident room as a constant reminder of my inability to block the inter-institutional "turf."

The NSx residents were fantastic to me. Once they saw that I could pull my weight doing scut on the floor during the day and handle my on-call duties reliably at night, I got to operate a lot. Aware of my OMS background, they assigned me to scrub in on relevant cases. I harvested an anterior iliac crest block bone graft for a cervical spine fusion case. I set the still-standing all-time record of performing eleven formal tracheostomies (not percutaneous) in one month. Unfortunately, there were many young, previously healthy, and predominantly male head trauma patients on service who were neurologically obtunded and ventilator-dependent status post GSW or MVA (motor vehicle accident). These patients required a trach and percutaneous endoscopic gastrostomy (PEG) feeding tube before transfer to a chronic neuro rehab center. With the assistance of an ICU nurse, I would trach these hemodynamically stable patients with anatomically ideal long, thin necks in the NSx ICU. It would serve as invaluable experience for my career-long "wonderful world of airway management."

Equally aware of my interest in upper facial third maxillofacial surgery, I was afforded the opportunity to scrub in on multiple craniotomy cases. I would perform the bicoronal flap (large scalp incision) with the NSx resident before he would proceed with the craniotomy and intracranial components of the operation. I would then close the bicoronal flap as the NSx resident would move on to the next case across the street. This too would serve as invaluable experience for bicoronal and hemicoronal approaches to frontal sinus and TMJ cases.

One Sunday morning, still in scrubs after operating all night with the NSx team, I drove over to Woodhull Hospital to serve as an OMS mock board examiner. Although our Greater New York OMS Mock Board serving fourteen residency programs would eventually move to Columbia, I kept my now thirty-three-year examiner streak intact. Even when I ultimately became an American Board of OMS (ABOMS) oral certification examiner, I maintained my commitment to that mock board.

Thanks in great part to my two months on the NSx service, we developed a collegial and symbiotic relationship between OMS and NSx that persists to this day. Frontal sinus fractures with posterior table involvement remain a joint venture. Intracranial infections of odontogenic etiology are managed jointly. Certainly, the field of craniofacial surgery offers a wonderful opportunity for cooperation between services.

~

In June, I rotated to the general surgery service at Long Island College Hospital (LICH), one of our private affiliate hospitals. This was twenty-three years before the 156-year-old SUNY-run hospital would be closed despite local community protests and Mayor Bill de Blasio's promise to keep it open. The hospital's position right off the Brooklyn Queens Expressway, with its reasonably priced adjoining modern parking garage, also made for a comfortable commute. A mix of Middle Eastern restaurants and eclectic bars offered top-notch lunch, dinner, and after-work options. Located in the gentrified Cobble Hill section of Brooklyn overlooking the Brooklyn Navy Yard, it was a fortuitous rotation during Fleet Week.

As for the service, it offered a broad spectrum of garden variety general surgery cases. It was a busy service with multiple attendings bringing in their private OR cases. Physician assistants (PAs) covered the scut work on the floor during the week, which freed the residents to operate all day long. It was fine except for Sundays, when residents were on-call without a PA. In the pre-ambulatory surgery era, all elective surgery patients were admitted the day before surgery for a full pre-op workup including labs, chest X-rays, EKG, consent and anesthesia clearance. It was common to have a dozen or more pre-ops to work up in addition to the ER admissions and floor patients to manage.

On-call every third night wasn't too tortuous. In exchange for a dozen Dunkin' Donuts, the overnight nursing staff afforded me two to three hours of sleep. Barring a true emergency requiring my immediate attention, they would make a list of all scut that arose overnight. They would wake me at five a.m. so I could hastily restart infiltrated IVs, draw morning blood tests, and change dressings before six a.m. rounds.

That arrangement worked fine until one graveyard shift when the head nurse abruptly woke me after completing her four a.m. TPR (temp, pulse, respiration) rounds. An eighty-year-old male with unresectable, metastatic pancreatic cancer was found unresponsive in his bed. I ran down the corridor to his room to find him pale, cold, and clammy. With no apparent pulse or respirations, he was unresponsive to pain or verbal commands. There was no telling if this was a recent event, since his condition might have deteriorated any time after twelve a.m. TPR rounds.

I was advised that the family had signed a do-not-resuscitate (DNR) order earlier that day; no need to run a code. But, I did have to fill out the death certificate stating the time and cause of death. While that seems like a simple enough task, no one wants to be the idiotic intern on-call who declares a patient dead only to have him wake up with a toe tag in the morgue. So, I found my trusty stethoscope and auscultated his heart and lungs and carotids for more than a minute to assure myself there was indeed no pulse or respiration. All that was left to do was contact the patient's attending physician, who was less than grateful for my call at five a.m. on a Sunday morning. No, I could be the one to notify the patient's family. Terrific. That call never gets easy.

My surgical experience at LICH was tailored to my OMS background. I scrubbed in on parotid and thyroid surgery with the highly respected chief of surgery, who would go on to become chairman at SUNY Downstate. I scrubbed in on midface fracture cases with the plastic surgeon covering facial trauma at their Level II trauma center. I even joined the OMS attendings on their private orthognathic cases and service mandible fractures. Although often feeling like a fish out of water operating in the abdomen, I immediately felt at home returning to the head and neck arena.

Just so happens, I was the resident on-call at LICH the last night of the gen surg resident academic year. The new incoming interns arrived at six a.m. on July 1. One by one, they gathered in the on-call room wearing their bright new, clean, long, white hospital coats with their stethoscopes in the pockets. They all shared that deer-in-the-headlights look as they were about to transition from medical student to physician/surgeon. "Who's the poor guy on-call tonight?" I asked on my way out the door. "Here's the beeper. Good luck with that."

~

Later that morning, I drove over the Verrazano-Narrows Bridge, connecting Brooklyn to Staten Island. When it opened in 1964, it was the world's longest suspension span at 2.5 miles. Today, it is the nation's most expensive bridge with a toll of $19 for non-Staten Island residents without an E-ZPass. From the Clove Road exit off the Staten Island Expressway, I took the local streets and arrived to start my next rotation at St. Vincent's Medical Center. At the time, it was a university-level affiliate of SUNY Brooklyn and a welcome rotation for all gen surg residents.

The Sisters of Charity Healthcare System ran St. Vincent's Hospital from 1903 until it closed in 2006. It reopened in its present incarnation in 2007 as Richmond University Medical Center, or RUMC, a Level I trauma center. As a private hospital, its attendings admitted their own patients for a wide variety of general surgical procedures. With competent nurses and PAs manning the floors, the residents were liberated to operate all day one-on-one with the attendings.

Overnight on-call was a different story. The ER was quite busy with a host of garden variety surgical admissions. One such night, I was the lucky recipient of not one, not two, but three appendectomies back to back to back. The senior resident handling consults in the ER evaluated all three acute appendicitis cases, and based on his clinical exams, he determined that surgery was in order. This was in the days before conservative treatment with IV antibiotics and observation was considered a viable option.

A relatively young patient with acute onset right lower quadrant pain made worse by palpation of the left lower abdomen (Rovsing's sign), fever, and an elevated white count was a candidate for emergent surgery. The Asian general surgeon on-call spoke little English. He was not a proponent of laparoscopic appendectomy, which was still in its infancy. Rather, he preferred an open approach via a small two- to three-inch incision over McBurney's point. With a series of grunts and hand gestures, he expertly guided me through the abdominal wall into the abdomen to find and remove the appendix. By our third case that night, on a ten-year-old boy, I completed the appendectomy in seventeen minutes from skin to skin. A "record" the general surgeon uttered as he stormed out of the OR.

After checking on my three post-ops in the recovery room, I retreated to the surgery on-call room around two a.m. It was located next door in the Sisters' Monastery. The room was spartan and clean. I fell asleep as soon as my head hit the flat hospital supply pillow. At three a.m., my beeper went off, startling me. I turned on the single lamp in the room located next to the bed and saw a huge white cross suspended from the corner ceiling. Culture shock for a Jewish guy.

Later that week, I presented those three appendectomy cases at grand rounds. The chief of surgery, a highly respected thoracic surgeon who ran his department with an iron fist, was in utter dismay. Casually, I mentioned that all three appendices were negative on histopathologic analysis. Continually tapping his head with his right hand, as was his habit when he was upset, he launched into me. He correctly claimed that a 20 percent false positive rate on appendectomy was acceptable to avoid the complications of a ruptured appendix such as peritonitis. But a 100 percent false positive rate was totally unacceptable. Who had made the final diagnoses? I couldn't hang my senior resident or attending out to dry. I took one for the team.

Then there was my "99"-themed grand rounds presentation at St. Vincent's. Another night on-call the following week, my chief resident and I were paged stat to the ER for a ninety-nine-year-old Black male trauma patient. Evidently, he had fallen and hit his head in the bathtub. The local nursing home had no DNR on record. Minimally responsive but with reasonably stable vital signs, anesthesia had intubated him in the ER to protect his airway. The ER MD had sutured his scalp laceration. Although significant head trauma in a ninety-nine-year-old patient is associated with greater than a 99 percent mortality rate, the decision was made to proceed with a head CT scan to rule out an intracranial bleed.

My CR and I accompanied the patient down the hall to radiology, where he was placed on a ventilator with appropriate monitors. Midway through the CT scan, the EKG monitor indicated asystole. We backed him out of the scanner immediately. There was no palpable pulse, so we halfheartedly started a cardiopulmonary resuscitation/advanced cardiac life support protocol. We declared him dead upon return to the ER. It only seemed appropriate that I wear a number "99" football jersey that I had purchased at a local sporting goods store to my grand rounds presentation. Once again, the chief could only tap his head as I recounted the case.

Aware of my history, the CR assigned me to cover all private oral surgery cases, so I got to scrub in with the chief of OMS at St. Vincent's. A well-respected Staten Island oral surgeon, he was equally well known as a Westminster Dog Show judge and Vizsla breeder.

One memorable patient was a seventy-year-old White woman who presented as an unrestrained driver in an MVA, sustaining a LeFort III fracture as her only significant injury. After appropriate clearances, we took her to the OR for an ORIF of her midface fractures. Since she was edentulous, we didn't have to place her in intermaxillary fixation or wire her jaws shut. Instead, we placed four titanium miniplates with sixteen screws intraorally to fixate the LeFort I horizontal fracture component. The attending told me to close the mucosal wound as he prepared to scrub out. At that point, I politely reminded him that we still had to stabilize the LeFort III fracture components to the next intact superior bones. Somewhat miffed, he inquired about my training. Once I informed him that I was an OMS attending at a Level I trauma center in my previous incarnation, he let me proceed with the four additional skin incisions and semirigid fixation. He was collegial and a perfect gentleman.

~

In August 1991, I returned to the County, which meant summer in the city. The dog days of summer meant a busy trauma rotation for me. The chief and senior residents operated all night long, leaving the trauma intern running the show in the ER. Sleep on-call was not even a possibility. The crack epidemic was still in full swing, ensuring the Kings County Knife and Gun Club would again be up and running like it was during my oral surgery trauma rotation. Eighteen trauma admissions a night was par for the course.

One Saturday night was particularly busy with a drug-based gang skirmish in full swing. It was like a MASH unit in a war zone. Multiple triaged GSW patients, who were reasonably stable, were backed up in the C-1 acute trauma area waiting their turn to go to the OR. It got so busy that the trauma team was running two ORs simultaneously. Word was sent down to me from my senior resident that I was to independently suture all stab wounds and major lacerations in the C-1 area. This of course excluded stab wounds to the abdomen with a positive diagnostic peritoneal lavage that necessitated exploratory laparotomy, or wounds to Zone II of the neck deep to the platysma muscle that required a neck exploration. Sidebar—Management of penetrating wounds to neck: Zone I-clavicle to cricoid-angiography, Zone II-cricoid to angle of mandible-surgical exploration, Zone III-angle of mandible to skull base-angiography. CTAngio was not yet in vogue for neck wounds.

With the assistance of the able C-1 nurses and my medical student, I had things reasonably under control until EMS brought in a twenty-year-old Black gangbanger. He was conscious but spurting blood from a deep vertical midline neck stab wound. The patient was tachycardic and moderately hypotensive. I packed the wound and started two large bore IVs for fluid resuscitation, which stabilized him. The trauma attending on-call came down from the OR. I was friends with him, having rotated on the trauma service together as residents ten years earlier during my oral surgery days. He glanced at the patient and nodded to me. "You're an OMS. You work in the neck. You do trachs. You can handle it here."

A nurse held a flashlight so I could better see the deep wound. With the patient awake and cursing me out, I administered local anesthesia to the periphery of the wound. My medical student assisted me with a portable Gomco suction. I removed the packing, and the wound immediately gushed bright-red blood, indicating an arterial bleed. A second medical student retracted the wound for me. With the added exposure, I could see that the wound extended deeply to the pre-tracheal fascia. I clamped the bleeding vessel, which appeared to be emanating from a branch off the superior thyroid artery. I ligated the artery with two 3x0 black silk ties. The hemorrhage stopped instantly. I irrigated the wound with normal saline and explored the depth. I asked the patient to take a deep breath. No bubbles were discernible, indicating the trachea had not been violated. I sutured the wound in layers, placed in a small drain, and applied a pressure dressing. I kept him overnight in the C-1 area for observation to rule out expanding hematoma or subcutaneous emphysema that could cause an urgent airway problem.

By six a.m., the entire trauma team arrived in the C-1 area to commence rounds. We had admitted twenty-four patients overnight and operated on six of them. The trauma chief of service could only shake his head when I presented my neck stab wound patient, saying, "Reminds me of Vietnam. That took balls." My attending friend laughed.

$\sim$

September meant a return to the main campus at University Hospital-Downstate Medical Center. The general surgery inpatient service was perched on the eighth floor, atop the hospital pyramid both figuratively and literally. It also housed the administrative offices of the Department of Surgery. Besides the chairman, several other academic surgeons operated at University Hospital.

During the day, I was assigned to general surgery, which was a relatively gentlemanly service. On-call overnight was a different story altogether. We cross-covered the transplant surgery service, which was torture. Transplant patients, mostly renal transplants on immunosuppressive meds, were advised to return to the ER for even the most mundane issues. A common cold would precipitate an admission for overnight observation to ward off any potential infection. The typical transplant patient would be accompanied by a shopping bag of medication bottles, all of which had to be reordered into the system. The simplest admission from the ER turned into an hour-long scutological assault.

Daytime, the first case I scrubbed in on at Downstate that rotation was an abdominoplasty. The middle-aged White woman had previously undergone a vertical banded gastroplasty (VBG), commonly referred to as stomach stapling, and had lost more than 100 pounds. She needed a panniculectomy or superficial abdominoplasty to remove excess skin and fat. The general surgeon who had performed the VBG was assisted by his colleague, a noted trauma surgeon at the County. He knew my background and told me to "Go for it."

They guided me as I used a #10 blade to make the extensive elliptical skin incision below the umbilicus, or belly button, from hip to hip. I continued the dissection with Bovie electrocautery through subcutaneous tissue and superficial fat. The attending was quick to clamp the arterial perforators as I proceeded the length of the incision. I doubled back to "buzz" the vessels. Unfortunately, the attending evidently removed one of the hemostats before I had cauterized that vessel. Immediately, blood shot up and somehow managed to get under my glasses and into my left eye. Embarrassed, I focused and reclamped the vessel, then placed a black silk tie to ligate it. Both attendings told me to scrub out immediately and rinse out my eye and wash my face. They advised me to go to Employee Health and document the incident as a possible HIV exposure. The trauma attending laughed as he added that "a splash in the eye was as good as a dick in the ass."

I proceeded to see the Employee Health Physician, a more reassuring type, who had been one of my internal medicine attendings during my medical school clerkship. In subsequent years, she would be helpful to our dual-degree program in her influential role on the medical school admissions committee. She thought my exposure risk was moderately low, especially since the patient was healthy with normal blood values. Still, she advised that I take a baseline HIV test and ask the patient to submit to one as well, once she was fully awake from her anesthetic. Turned out that the patient did have one known risk factor for HIV because she had received multiple blood transfusions in the past. I was advised to start an antiviral cocktail immediately until I knew the patient's status. In the early 1990s, there was no HIV quick test and results took the better part of a week. The cocktail was rather toxic, and after two days, I bailed out. Fortunately, we both tested negative. Interestingly, not much concern was raised about the risk of Hepatitis C in those days; certainly it would be of concern today. Then again, her liver enzymes were normal, and there was no treatment for it anyway.

~

One relatively peaceful Sunday night on-call, as I was prepping for my ATLS course the next day, the charge nurse frantically paged me. It seemed that a post-op patient had pulled out her NGT. This would be no big deal except that it was the chair's private patient, who had just undergone a Billroth II gastrojejunostomy. This procedure involved partial gastrectomy (removal of the distal stomach), often for cancer, and anastomosis of the gastric stump to the jejunum (small intestine). The NGT was essential to prevent retention of gastric secretions or reflux in the early post-op period while the anastomosis healed awaiting return of normal bowel function.

I was well aware that the chair only wanted the chief resident in-house to perform interventions on his patients. Unfortunately, the CR supposedly in-house was MIA. So, much to the chagrin of the nurse and against the objections of the patient, I carefully passed the NGT with care to avoid damage to the anastomosis. I auscultated with my stethoscope to assure proper tube placement and doubly confirmed tip position with a radiograph.

Everything was fine until morning rounds. The chair went positively ballistic when I informed the team that I had replaced the NGT overnight. I covered for the chief resident when asked why I hadn't contacted him. I merely replied that as an OMS, I routinely placed NGTs in many of our patients to bypass the oral cavity to facilitate wound healing or to prevent aspiration of stomach contents in our patients who were in intermaxillary fixation.

Later that day, the chairman summoned me to his office. I anxiously entered his expansive, stately furnished space. Rather than chastise me further, he offered me a categorical position in the general surgery program on the spot. At thirty-eight years old, and mindful of my promise to my wife, I politely declined the offer. It would be time to return to gainful employment in five months as a dual-degree OMS. He did give me an "excellent" on my resident evaluation at the end of the rotation.

～

I returned to Kings County Hospital in October and November for two additional months on the tumor and vascular surgery services. I was now a veteran on the tumor service and comfortable at the County. I had become quite experienced at "needle loc" mammography-aided breast biopsies as well as other lump and bump minor surgeries.

One day, I was summoned across the street to the Downstate OR to assist on an excision of a submandibular gland. The private gen surg attending, younger than myself, had been one of my medical students when I rotated on the trauma service as an OMS resident ten years before. He was aware of my OMS training and handed me the scalpel. He concurred when I pointed out the lingual nerve as it sprang up into the floor of the mouth upon completion of one of my favorite anatomic dissections. He commented that I appeared much more comfortable operating in the neck than the abdomen. He was correct, indeed.

The vascular surgery service wasn't as rewarding as the tumor service for the interns. The good cases such as the fem-pop (femoral-popliteal arterial bypass surgery) were reserved for the more senior residents.

One night on-call around two a.m., we emergently took a sixty-year-old White male with a history of poorly controlled diabetes and advanced peripheral vascular disease to the OR for amputation of a gangrenous foot. He had become septic and was so hypotensive that Anesthesia refused to administer general anesthesia. They gave him a few milligrams of morphine and advised us to "hurry up." My CR had originally done his gen surg training in Lebanon and served in their Army during the Israeli-Lebanese conflict. Amputation was a chip shot for him. There was no time for the more complex below-knee or trans-tibial amputation, so we had to perform a guillotine knee disarticulation. My CR handed me a #10 blade and told me I had thirty seconds or he was going to take over. I completed the amputation with ten seconds to spare. I looked up to see the popliteal artery spurting blood clear across the OR, hitting the back wall. I clamped the vessel and double ligated it. After some minor soft tissue work, we packed the stump. We were done in five minutes. The patient survived the procedure.

~

The Brooklyn VA was the ideal rotation for December. Commute wise, it was the easiest hospital to get to in Brooklyn since it was right off the Verrazano Bridge. With the holidays approaching, most of the inpatients couldn't wait to be discharged to go home for the holidays. I arrived with a census of twenty-four patients on my surgical floor. Within a week, I had knocked it down to a mere two inpatients. As a bonus, since the census was so light and most of the surgical attendings took off for the holidays, we split the surgical team in half. One half of the team had Christmas week off, and the other half was off for New Year's week. Since I hadn't had a vacation day since I started my surgery residency year in April, I welcomed the opportunity to spend

Christmas week with my family.

One interesting facet of the VA was the first-floor commissary. It sold cigarettes at incredibly low prices to the veterans, outpatients and inpatients alike. One night on-call, I went to perform a routine post-op check on an ENT patient with a fifty pack-year smoking history. He had undergone a laryngectomy earlier that day for advanced laryngeal cancer. Surprisingly, he was not in his bed. I found him in the bathroom smoking a cigarette through his new tracheostomy tube. I sternly admonished him to stop smoking. He gave me the finger.

The month was low-key. I got to do a bunch of inguinal hernias on the all-male veteran patient population. In the surgical lexicon, it's been said that it takes fifty inguinal hernia cases before one fully comprehends the operation. I'm not sure I ever attained that level of comprehension.

Working on New Year's week, I had one major avoidable complication. A frail seventy-five-year-old White woman, a rare female patient at the VA, was scheduled for a left lobectomy for lung cancer. The thoracic surgery attending had requested that she be transferred to the SICU for pre-op optimization. This meant a central line for better venous access and an arterial line for intraoperative BP monitoring as well as arterial blood draws. My senior resident and I debated which side to place the central line. We decided to place a right subclavian line, leaving a virgin left hemithorax for the planned surgery. WRONG!

Unfortunately, under the watchful guidance of my senior resident, I atraumatically placed the right subclavian line. Or so I thought. I was really proud of myself until we viewed the requisite post-placement chest X-ray. I had dropped her right lung! I got another procedure out of it; I placed a right chest tube to treat the iatrogenic pneumothorax. I called the thoracic attending and informed him of the development. He went ballistic on me. He explained that he would be dropping the left lung to perform the lobectomy. Anesthesia would be using a double lumen endotracheal tube and needed an intact right lung to ventilate the patient. He would have to postpone the surgery until the right lung was totally re-expanded, the pneumothorax resolved, and the chest tube was out. The patient and her family were not very happy with me. My senior resident, a great guy who would go on into pediatric urology, took the hit for me at rounds the next morning.

I had the misfortune of being on-call New Year's Eve. Everything was quiet at the VA, so the very same senior resident and I ventured into Bay Ridge for dinner at Griswold's Pub. It was on Third Avenue, a mere ten-minute drive from the hospital. We had just finished our burgers when we were both paged simultaneously from the ER—not a good sign. We rushed back in five minutes, blowing through multiple red lights.

In the ER, we found a fifty-five-year-old White male veteran who was a smoker but otherwise had no significant past medical, surgical, or family history. He complained of new onset acute abdominal pain radiating to his back. A physical exam revealed a palpable periumbilical thrill. My senior resident and I nodded; it had to be an abdominal aortic aneurysm (AAA). We accompanied him to radiology for an emergent CT of the abdomen/pelvis with contrast. We were shocked to see that this previously healthy middle-aged man had a 6.5-centimeter AAA. His blood pressure was difficult to control with various antihypertensive meds, and we were leery of an impending rupture. I met with the patient and his family to discuss his options while my senior tried to find a VA vascular surgeon available on New Year's Eve.

As the ball dropped at midnight in Times Square, we entered the OR. In 1992, endovascular repair of AAAs was not commonplace. So, for the next four hours, I retracted for the open abdominal surgery. This included keeping pressure on the infrarenal aorta proximal to the aneurysm. This allowed the vascular attending to minimize aortic cross-clamping time while he sutured the graft in place. My senior and I closed the long abdominal incision and took the patient to the recovery room by dawn.

I scarfed down coffee and a donut before going to speak with the family in the waiting room. Before I could notify them that the operation went as planned, I heard a "Code 99" called in the recovery room. I ran back to the RR to see the anesthesia team running a full code on our patient. I took over chest compressions. An arterial blood gas revealed that he was grossly acidotic, with a pH of 6.91 despite our efforts to minimize cross-clamping. Bicarb was administered to no avail. Time of death? Six thirty a.m. on New Year's Day.

Since I had established a rapport with the family, it was left to me to give them the terrible news. I notified them that the patient sustained a cardiac arrest in the recovery room. Despite our aggressive efforts, he could not be resuscitated. I offered my sincerest condolences. The wife and two teenage daughters were in shock. They couldn't fathom how their husband and father was seemingly in perfect health earlier New Year's Eve, only to be dead by New Year's morning. Exhausted, I walked to my car.

$$\sim$$

Nineteen ninety-two started with a fairly benign rotation on the pediatric surgery service (peds surg) at the County. Every third night, I was on-call in the children's receiving ward (CRW), mostly suturing an array of lacerations. I was even on-call the Sunday night of the Super Bowl, though I snuck away intermittently and watched the game in the adjacent B building pharmacy waiting room.

The CRW nurses were fantastic at managing hysterical young kids. The head nurse, who would soon retire, had a plaque raised in her name outside the treatment room to recognize her work. Whether it required TLC, a papoose board for restraint (with parental consent of course), or IM sedation, she was a master at pediatric patient management. I knew her well from many nights during my OMS intern year when she would page me and tell me to "bring my pullers" to the CRW, referencing our pediatric forceps used to extract mobile primary teeth.

Night call on peds surg also involved scut work on the B-91/B-92 pediatric wards. Drawing blood and restarting IVs in the middle of the night on uncooperative toddlers was both time consuming and totally exasperating for all involved—until I developed my secret weapon, that is. I would simply suggest to the recalcitrant kiddie that he (or she) sit still if he wanted to see his mother in the morning. This may sound cruel, but it was totally effective and humane in a way. It would save the kid needless unsuccessful venipuncture attempts. The only downside was that when our team would round on the ward at seven a.m., all the kids would cry when they saw me enter the room.

Pediatric trauma patients involved in MVAs, pedestrians struck while running into the street, and bicyclists hit by cars were more problematic. Brought in by EMS with a pediatric cervical collar in place and with their hysterical parents by their side, young children often required sedation for any indicated head and body CT scans. This necessitated intubation by anesthesia. I would then have to accompany the child to radiology, where a respiratory therapist was waiting for ventilator support during the CT scan. This was time dependent and occasionally stressful if the endotracheal tube was dislodged during transport. Fortunately, my four months of anesthesia training during my OMS residency paid off.

Peds surg offered a great opportunity to operate on a multitude of intern-level cases. The service was busy, operating Monday, Wednesday, and Friday at the County, then Tuesday and Thursday at Downstate. Typically, we would schedule eight cases on OR day at the County, including circumcisions, hernias, lumps, bumps, and even tongue-ties. Why peds surg performed ankyloglossia cases instead of OMS or even ENT defied my imagination, but I was more than happy to do them.

One venerable peds surg attending was even known to grab a mop himself to help clean OR #5 between cases to expedite turnover. Performing a circumcision with him was a joy to behold. He would call out the very same instructions each step of the case, regardless if it was the first or eighth such procedure of the day. "Hold that clamp on the foreskin for fifty-four seconds." At the completion of the case, he would announce to everyone in the room, "Perfect. Someday, some young lady will appreciate your work."

Unfortunately, I suffered two missteps during my peds surg rotation. One day on team rounds at the County with the peds surg fellow, I got my comeuppance, and rightly so. The fellowship position at Kings County-Downstate was one of only twenty-four such slots in the entire country at the time. The fellow, a supposed legend during his general surgery days at Mount Sinai, was fortunate to land the position. We stopped at the bed of a lovely five-year-old girl I had admitted the night before. I briefly presented the case to the team in front of her. She was pre-op for exploration of a recurrent abdominal sarcoma. We left her crying. Once in the hallway, the fellow reamed me a new asshole saying, "Don't ever assume that a five-year-old cancer patient doesn't understand what you're saying." Although at least five years younger than me, and equally cynical and sarcastic as me, I had to admit he was right. I had become institutionalized.

My other setback occurred in the OR at Downstate. I was operating with the chief of pediatric surgery on a five-year-old Black child who presented with an umbilical hernia. More common in Black infants than White infants, most umbilical hernias heal on their own by age four. In this case, the defect was fairly sizable and had not spontaneously closed, so the decision was reached with the parents to repair it. Having already done several inguinal hernias with the chief, he seemed at ease guiding me through this surgery. I made a three centimeter incision at the base of the umbilicus, detached the umbilical stalk, and identified the hernia sac. I then reduced the intestine and excised the sac. I closed the defect in the fascia with several sutures. It was now time to close the skin incision. Holy shit! I had inexplicably excised the umbilicus. The attending was speechless; gratefully, he didn't go ballistic on me. He directed me to suture the skin flaps down to the muscle layer and pack the wound to recreate a belly button.

To this day, I still don't have a clue how I did it. Every time I saw him thereafter, he would just shake his head in utter disbelief. But the peds surg chief, always the gentleman, would still be kind enough a few years later to serve as one of my initial references for a fellowship in the American College of Surgeons.

~

February 1992 approached. I had one month to go before my nonstop, no-vacation year of general surgery would be over. I was assigned to the SICU at Kings County. In 1992, the Accreditation Council for Graduate Medical Education restricted SICU coverage to second-year gen surg residents and their more senior counterparts. Since I had completed a three-year OMS residency and was about to complete my first gen surg year, I was deemed competent to run an eighteen-bed SICU by myself on-call. Theoretically, there was always a trauma chief resident in-house as back up, assuming he or she wasn't too busy in the OR. Coincidentally, I had an OMS rotator on-call with me every third night.

Days in the SICU started at six a.m. We scurried to draw morning labs and blood gases and order chest X-rays so they would be available for eight a.m. rounds with our entire team. The team included two other second-year gen surg residents and a fourth-year gen surg resident who was in charge of the unit. There were fourteen beds in the SICU, with an additional four beds allocated to us for boarders in the recovery room. The nursing care in the unit was outstanding, with each critical care nurse assigned to two adjacent patients per shift. A different attending oversaw the SICU each week and presided over afternoon rounds with the team. These attendings, including three trauma surgeons and one anesthesiologist, had pursued additional training at the finest trauma/critical care fellowships in the country, namely Maryland Shock Trauma and Jackson Memorial, in Miami.

The day shift flew by every day. Often, arrest codes interrupted morning rounds. The on-call teams became quite proficient at keeping the patients alive overnight by administering pressor support medication to maintain blood pressure and adjusting respirator settings to maintain adequate ventilatory support. There was no shortage of central lines, Swan-Ganz catheters, arterial lines, and chest tubes to place. There were ventilator-dependent patients to escort to radiology for X-rays and CT scans. We consulted with the patients' primary treating services, although we were ultimately responsible for their management while in the unit. The post-call resident could go home once the morning scut work and daily procedures were completed.

It was a fascinating opportunity to learn real life cardiopulmonary physiology. That was until six p.m., when the team completed evening rounds and swiftly departed. That left the on-call resident, namely me, with the daunting task of running an eighteen-bed unit by myself. Fuck me! Nineteen ninety-two just happened to be a leap year, and sure enough, I was the unlucky resident on-call the extra night. I had made it through the entire month without nuking anyone. One night to go!

A second-year OMS rotator was on-call with me that fateful night. He would go on to become one of my first and best residents that I would have the honor of training after returning as director of the OMS residency program. That last night in the unit, we were both just trying to get through unscathed.

It was a relatively quiet night except for one minor problem. We had an open SICU bed, meaning we could get an admission at any time. Of course, we got an absolute disaster. At midnight, the vascular service drop-kicked into the unit a sixty-year-old cachectic Black male with a history of coronary artery disease, poorly controlled hypertension, uncontrolled insulin dependent diabetes, end stage renal disease, and advanced peripheral vascular disease. He presented for pre-op optimization. This was prior to a planned below-knee amputation (BKA) of a gangrenous right lower extremity in the morning. "Tune him up," they cackled as they transferred him from his stretcher to his new unit bed. He would need an A-line, Foley bladder catheter, and the dreaded Swan-Ganz catheter.

The Swan-Ganz catheter, or pulmonary artery catheter, was popular in the 1980s as an invasive form of cardiac monitoring in the ICU setting. Most often, it is passed through the right internal jugular vein, through the superior vena cava to the right atrium then right ventricle of the heart, and finally into the pulmonary artery. It was an advanced diagnostic tool used to determine cardiogenic shock, pulmonary hypertension, intracardiac shunts, hemodynamic status, cardiac output, and pulmonary capillary wedge pressure. Therapeutically, it was used to maximize the effect of inotropic cardiac drugs. The procedure to place the catheter was not without risk of arrythmias, pseudoaneurysm or vessel rupture, thrombosis, sepsis, pneumothorax, and bleeding. Sidebar- the Swan-Ganz fell into disfavor by the turn of the century to be replaced by minimally invasive technology such as transesophageal echocardiography. Currently, totally noninvasive systems like the NICOM—noninvasive cardiac output monitoring—are often preferred.

I contacted the trauma CR to advise him that I was placing a Swan-Ganz catheter in this very sick patient. He was busy with a gunshot wound case in the OR and told me to go for it. The patient was pleasant enough but totally petrified of the procedure. After obtaining his reluctant consent, I administered two milligrams of morphine, prepped and draped him, and adjusted the monitors. With surprising ease, I introduced the balloon catheter into the right internal jugular vein. My OMS resident dutifully checked the EKG monitor as I carefully advanced the catheter through the right atrium into the right ventricle. Suddenly, we lost the EKG tracing on the monitor; all we saw was a flatline. "Check the leads!" I yelled. He went under the drapes and announced, "The leads are still on." "Fuck it." The catheter tip must have irritated the right ventricle, causing an arrythmia. I quickly pulled back the catheter, and sinus rhythm reappeared on the monitor. The OMS resident confirmed a palpable femoral pulse. What the hell; in for a penny, in for a pound. I tried it again, and this time I successfully advanced the catheter into the pulmonary artery. I sutured the line in place on the neck and shot our first cardiac outputs.

The patient, although still sedated, was responsive. Vitals were reasonably stable. To cover my ass, I obtained a stat cardiology consult. I ordered serial EKGs and cardiac enzymes to rule out a myocardial infarct. With his angina history, cardiology started him on a prophylactic nitroglycerine drip. Amazingly, the patient would survive his urgent surgery later that morning.

On six a.m. rounds, I recounted the night's events. The SICU chief resident congratulated me on making it through the month with no clean kills. I thanked the nurses for their help as I left the SICU. I felt an adrenaline rush as I exited the hospital and walked to my car. At thirty-nine years old, I had survived two years of medical school and a year of general surgery residency. I had completed it all in thirty-two months. As I drove through Brooklyn, I stopped at a tobacco store on the corner of Flatbush and Atlantic, the future site of the Barclays Center twenty years hence. I bought the biggest Macanudo cigar in the store. I smoked it as I drove over the Brooklyn Bridge, up FDR Drive, and over the George Washington Bridge into New Jersey. It was time to start the next chapter of my career.

Director I: 1992–2000

AFTER TAKING MARCH 1992 off to rest and recuperate on another obligatory trip to Florida with my wife and kids, it was time to focus on my career. Multiple discussions over the past three years with my chairman of Dental and Oral and Maxillofacial Surgery had established my future role in the department. Now, it was time to enact those plans.

First, I was named co-director of the OMS residency program with my mentor, Dr. Bernard Gold. He was not too pleased to share the position with me. He saw me as overly ambitious and a threat to his authority. To make matters worse for him, we were cited for not having a full-time director of OMS during the American Dental Association (ADA) mandated five-year site visit in fall 1992. Since he still ran a full-time private practice on Pitkin Avenue in Brooklyn, he reluctantly relinquished his title by spring 1993, thereby making me full-time director of the OMS residency program. Ultimately, he would resign to take the OMS residency director position at Columbia in 1994.

More importantly, I went from a half-time slot to a full-time pay line at double the salary, with full benefits and a pension plan. My chairman took advantage of my return to expand the residency program to cover maxillofacial trauma at both Coney Island Hospital and Brookdale Medical Center. Coupled with a part-time pay line at Maimonides Medical Center and a modest faculty practice at Downstate Medical Center, I generated an income comparable to what I had been making before my departure from private practice. Little did I know then that my pension from Kings County would enable me to retire comfortably twenty-six years later at the age of sixty-five.

Being somewhat naïve and inexperienced, I accepted the

entry-level academic title of assistant professor of surgery at SUNY Downstate College of Medicine. While hard to imagine at the time, it would take me twelve years, twenty-one publications in peer-reviewed journals, four book chapters, and countless local, national, and international lectures before I would be promoted to the rank of full professor in 2004. Of course, serving as only the twenty-eighth OMS in the country to be inducted as a Fellow in the American College of Surgeons in 1996 certainly helped.

My first couple of years as OMS program director were interesting to say the least. Appreciative of the residents, I subsidized pizza at our weekly lunch and learns, coffee and donuts at our Wednesday afternoon implant conferences, and soda and munchies at our Thursday five p.m. grand rounds. Of course, the menu was somewhat limited by the fact that the pizza place, Dunkin' Donuts, and the corner deli were the only edible establishments on Clarkson Avenue.

Then, there was the constant tension between the chairman and me. This internal battle was waged over the surgical direction of the program. Being dual-degreed and dual-licensed, plus with a year of general surgery and two months of neurosurgery training under my belt, I was ready to expand the scope of our program. This aspirational expansion would include: performing tracheostomies, bicoronal flaps for frontal sinus fractures, and harvesting anterior and posterior iliac crest bone grafts (hip), calvaria grafts (skull), tibia grafts (lower leg), and costochondral grafts (rib). The chairman, who was reluctant to rock the boat at the medical board staffed by his cronies, offered initial resistance but ultimately acquiesced to my demands. Of course, I had to guarantee that I could perform these expanded scope procedures better than those other services we had consulted to perform in the past.

Tension also existed within our admissions committee, which consisted mainly of the chairman and me, over the ranking of several applicants. We conducted probably the worst interviews on the circuit, a fact later confirmed by applicants we had interviewed but matched at other programs. Every five minutes, the chairman, who felt it imperative to take every phone call his duty-bound secretary announced via overhead intercom, would interrupt the interview.

Logistically, the program underwent several changes during these early years. In 1993, we transitioned from a three-year program to a four-year certificate program. This meant our chief resident at the time was cordially invited to stay for a second CR year. His co-chief became our first six-year MD/OMS resident to matriculate in the program. To adequately staff our clinic, as the MD/OMS residents left for three years in the middle of residency to complete medical school and general surgery, we had to do some juggling. We requested and received a five-year waiver from the Commission on Dental Accreditation (CODA) of the ADA to increase our first-year enrollment from two to four residents. During this time, we accepted two four-year OMS certificate residents and two six-year MD/OMS residents, graduating three residents total per year. In subsequent years up to the present, once this system was already established, we matriculated three residents per year, including two MD/OMS residents and one four-year OMS certificate resident. We also hired a one-year preliminary OMS intern to ensure adequate manpower to run the clinic.

In the early years of the dual-degree program, we suffered some attrition. Once in medical school or general surgery, our residents excelled and were highly recruited by other services. We lost two residents to anesthesia, one to emergency medicine, and one to orthopedics. Two residents were poached by other supposed top-shelf OMS programs to fill openings after their own residents transferred. In subsequent years, with the assistance of the medical school, we dissuaded residents from jumping ship. We emphasized at the initial interview that our dual-degree residents were attending medical school as a member of an integrated six-year program. They were not free agents but had made a six-year commitment to complete our program. Also, with the medical health insurance crunch and the advent of lucrative implant practices, OMS became very financially rewarding and our retention rate improved. However, if a fully matriculated resident expressed a desire to seek additional training *after* completion of our program, then we would support their endeavors. In fact, three such residents went on to complete a required second year of general surgery prior to pursuing plastic surgery residency and craniofacial surgery fellowship.

Interestingly enough, my first four-year resident, Dr. Steven Izzo, would go on to become our outstanding associate program director throughout my tenure at the County. During his mandated second CR year in 1993, we took a road trip to Nashville, Tennessee, for a TMJ conference at the Opryland Hotel. The TMJ conference was interesting enough. More importantly, my CR and I developed a fondness for Lynchburg lemonades. Lynchburg, Tennessee, is the home of the Jack Daniel's Tennessee Whiskey distillery.

We were also indoctrinated into country music. Music City was in the midst of its revitalization as the country music capital of the world. We attended a concert at the Grand Ole Opry, where we saw Garth Brooks and Vince Gill perform. I also contacted my former CR from back in my OMS intern days who had gone on to medical school and plastic surgery. He was now director of craniofacial surgery at Vanderbilt. Little did I know then that it would be only the first of many trips for me to Nashville, a great town. Eighteen years later, my older daughter would enter Vanderbilt Medical School. Unfortunately, upon our return to the County, our chairman fought us tooth and nail on our expense report.

UNREQUITED LOVE

Two memorable clinical cases at the start of my director years, in the early 1990s, shared dramatic maxillofacial repercussions. Both cases involved unsuccessful suicide attempts after the patients' girlfriends terminated their relationships—unrequited love. Both patients suffered and survived devastating penetrating maxillofacial injuries, underwent multiple complex surgeries, received extensive psychiatric care, and had surprising endings.

The first such case, in 1993, involved a Middle Eastern young man who was distraught over his long-term girlfriend's unilateral decision to break off their relationship. He confronted her and threatened to kill himself if she left him. She tried to de-escalate the situation, but to no avail. He pulled out a .45-caliber pistol and, in the police vernacular, "ate his gun." As is often the case, he flinched at the very last moment as he squeezed the trigger. This caused the bullet to track right of midline and shatter his right mandible, maxilla, zygoma, and orbit.

Somehow, he survived his failed suicide attempt, and EMS took him to Kings County. After an emergency tracheostomy in the ER, the OMS team took him to the OR for the first of what would turn out to be a dozen trauma and reconstructive surgeries. The initial eight-hour surgery included debridement of shattered teeth and bones, reduction and fixation of the facial fractures where possible, soft tissue approximation of the cheek, and enucleation of the ruptured globe by ophthalmology. Over the next few years, other surgeries included bone grafts to reconstruct his right lateral maxillary wall and orbital floor for a conformer prior to globe prosthesis, lysis of his right TMJ ankylosis, a temporalis flap to close his large oro-antral defect, and local skin flaps to improve the cheek scar.

Over the years, for each surgery he returned, accompanied by his sister, with a large wall clock that he would position at the foot of his hospital bed. Miraculously, he was neurologically grossly intact, except for a gait disturbance necessitating a cane and an unusual finding on the clock-drawing test. This spatial planning deficit, often due to traumatic brain injury, resulted from nondominant right parietal impairment and left hemispace neglect. When asked to draw a clock like the one at the foot of his bed, he would draw one with all twelve numbers aligned on the right side. When he would emerge from a general anesthetic, to check his neuro status I would tap his right hand and ask him to show me two fingers. I knew he had returned to his baseline when he gave me the middle finger of both hands.

After his last scheduled surgery, he was lost to follow-up for over a decade. One day, he reappeared out of nowhere, with his sister, to say hello. He informed me that he had just returned from Yemen, where he had been living until a civil war forced him to flee to the US. He smiled when he showed me a photo of his new bride. Congratulations, Clock Man!

The second such case presented in 1996. A young White male was distraught after his fiancée informed him that she was breaking off the engagement. Since it was the July 4th weekend, he ran to his garage and returned with an M-80 firecracker in his mouth. He threatened to light the fuse if she left him. When she started to walk away, he detonated the pyrotechnic device. Urban legend has it that the explosive in an M-80 is equivalent to a quarter stick of dynamite.

The centrifugal force of the explosion was overwhelming but confined to midline structures. EMS took him to the County in surprisingly stable hemodynamic and neurological condition. He had sustained a LeFort II fracture, avulsive mandibular fracture, and degloving soft tissue injuries. Plastic surgery was covering maxillofacial trauma call that day but asked for OMS assistance. We gladly agreed to split the case since all the midface fractures were bilateral in nature.

After appropriate consults and trauma clearance, we took him to the OR for a two-team joint surgical approach. Somehow, he had been orally intubated in the ER, which we converted to a trach. We debrided shattered teeth and bone and reduced multiple fractures and fixated them with miniplates where adequate bone remained. The orbital floors were reconstructed after ophtho had ruled out globe rupture. The centrifugal wounds that had appeared to be grossly avulsive were able to be reapproximated with minimal soft tissue loss. We took the patient directly to the SICU after his twelve-hour surgery.

His post-op course was fairly unremarkable but prolonged. Psychiatric care was continued until he was deemed to no longer be a danger to himself. OMS performed multiple secondary reconstructive surgeries, including bone grafts to alveolar defects, local flap closure of his oro-antral defect, dental implants, and nasal reconstruction. One day prior to discharge, our OMS team was summoned to his room.

Pleasantly surprised, we all witnessed his bedside wedding ceremony to his former fiancée, now wife. Congratulations, M-80 man!

UNDER ATTACK

Spring 1994 started memorably for my wife and me with the birth of our son, Zachary, on April 7. In subsequent years, his birthday would run the gamut weather wise. One year on his birthday, he would pitch in eighty-degree heat; another year, a blizzard landed with a foot of snow—maybe the forerunner of global warming?

In early fall 1994, I attended the American Association of Oral and Maxillofacial Surgeons (AAOMS) Annual Meeting in Orlando, Florida, with my two new chief residents. My chairman and I had established a new policy that would remain in effect for the next twenty-four years during my tenure as program director. If the CRs produced either a poster or oral abstract accepted for presentation at the AAOMS Annual Meeting, then we would sponsor their trip. This included reimbursement of airfare, transfers, and hotel fees but not food or entertainment. I, as program director, would represent the Kings County Hospital OMS residency program at the faculty section meeting held the Thursday morning of the Annual Meeting. The program would reimburse me, on a tight budget, as well.

My first faculty section meeting was quite an eye-opener. Representatives, usually chairmen or program directors, were in attendance from most of the 108 OMS programs in existence at the time. Voting members received a laminated placard upon signing in. Green represented an affirmative vote on one side and red a negative vote on the other. Little did I know that I would be the subject of such a vote later in the meeting. When the meeting had proceeded to new business, the chairman of the Louisville program proposed an out-of-nowhere motion to shut down the Kings County Hospital OMS residency program. He claimed that a dentist, not an OMS, was running the program. Furthermore, he reported that Kings County's OMS program director, referring to Dr. Gold, was only part-time and merely a figurehead. This was in violation of the ADA's CODA accreditation standards and the AAOMS faculty section guidelines.

Not known for my diplomacy, I went ballistic. Urged on by members of the New York contingent, I raised my hand and was granted the floor for rebuttal. I stood up and approached this fine Kentucky gentleman. I assured him that I was the recently appointed full-time OMS program director at Kings County-SUNY Downstate. Furthermore, I had no intention of being anyone's stooge, including my chairman's. Yes, it was true, especially in the New York City Health and Hospitals Corporation system, that a general dentist often chaired the dental department. However, I assured the group that I had full autonomy to run the OMS division. In fact, I was a dual-degreed, dual-licensed, board-certified OMS and was only too happy to put my credentials up against anyone's in the room.

No one seconded the motion; it was quickly tabled. After the meeting, several newfound colleagues approached me and offered their support. But what if I hadn't been at the meeting to protect our program? It was far better to have nipped the process in the bud than to fight the ADA and AAOMS after the fact.

Unbeknownst to me, while being attacked at the faculty section meeting, my two CRs were summoned by the executive secretary of AAOMS. She grilled them about our program's leadership. They confirmed my claims. My chairman never knew I had saved the OMS program that day. I celebrated that night with my CRs at a strip club on the Orange Blossom Trail.

One of those two chief residents went on to become the butt of a hilarious practical joke at our year-end outing at the chairman's country club. After the morning guest lecture, we reconvened in the banquet hall for lunch. Those of us playing golf in the afternoon then had to pass through the members' dining room on the way to the men's locker room. Lo and behold, who did we happen to see having lunch with one of the members but Joe DiMaggio.

"Joltin' Joe" the "Yankee Clipper" was eighty and appeared quite frail. Certainly, he looked nothing like the Hall of Fame Yankee center-fielder whose fifty-six-game hitting streak remains intact some eighty years later. Surely not the handsome husband of Marilyn Monroe in the early 1950s nor the "Mr. Coffee" spokesman on TV commercials in the 1970s.

DiMaggio was big on the burgeoning sports memorabilia circuit in the 1980s. Even today, a Joe DiMaggio signed baseball is valued at around $500. It was widely known that he did not welcome autograph seekers invading his privacy. So, we all stayed clear of his table as we passed through, but word spread like wildfire that "Joe D" was in the house.

One of the general practice dental residents came up with a great idea for a practical joke on the somewhat gullible CR. Since the GPR wasn't playing golf or tennis, he drove to the local mall and stopped in the sporting goods store to purchase a Rawlings Official Major League baseball. In his best handwriting, he forged DiMaggio's autograph on the ball.

After dinner, all the GPRs presented the chief resident with the autographed baseball as a graduation gift. The CR was ecstatic as he showed all of us the ball. None of us had the heart to tell him it was a practical joke . . . until the next day, when he went ballistic. A very good guy nonetheless.

∼

The ADA and AAOMS would attempt to close the County program again. Evidently, they had conducted a manpower study and determined that 108 programs nationally were producing too many oral surgeons, which would potentially saturate the job market by the new millennium. They set about to systematically close several programs by establishing stricter graduation requirements.

Accreditation standards were increased to at least ten major cases per graduating CR in four distinct categories: trauma, pathology, reconstruction (including cosmetic surgery), and orthognathics. Inner-city programs based at Level I trauma centers, like Kings County, had no problem fulfilling the trauma and pathology requirements. However, elective cases in the cosmetic and orthognathic categories were often problematic. With three graduating CRs, thirty orthognathic cases per year was our major hurdle. Orthognathics is the surgical correction of skeletal dentofacial deformities such as mandibular prognathism or retrognathia and midface excess or deficiency. Unlike orthodontics, which involves the movement of the dentition, orthognathics involves skeletal repositioning. Other programs based their prodigious numbers on private cases brought in from the community by their private attendings. Their residents would often assist and retract for these attendings, who actually performed the surgery. While our numbers may have been fewer, at least our service cases were worked up, operated on, and followed up by the residents under attending supervision.

By the time of our next ADA CODA accreditation site visit in 1997 (on a five-year cycle), we had fulfilled all surgical case requirements. The program was running smoothly, so I anticipated no problems—a bit naïve on my part. Unbeknownst to me, the ADA CODA had no intention of conducting a fair residency review. The site visitors didn't simply interview my staff and residents, they interrogated them.

At the mandatory debriefing, with the chairman, hospital CEO, and myself present, the site visitors rattled off a startling total of sixteen recommendations. These here-to-fore unheard of "recommendations" were in fact citations that had to be corrected to the ADA's satisfaction within two years or the program would lose its accreditation and be forced to close.

The report left my chair, the CEO, and me aghast. Most of the sixteen citations were utter nonsense or total falsehoods. I sent a scathing critique of the site visitors to the ADA but to no avail. The program was demoted to provisional status. It would take me the better part of the next two years to satisfactorily address all sixteen citations. The time I spent on this administrative nonsense took me away from my surgical and resident training duties. It hurt the program rather than helped it. By 1999, we had regained full accreditation status.

Somehow, I successfully navigated the next four site visits, in 2002, 2007, 2012, and 2017, with a grand total of only four recommendations. All four recs were corrected before the site visitors had even boarded their planes home. In fact, we received zero recommendations during my last two site visits as program director in 2012 and 2017.

Ironically, a couple of years after the 1997 debacle, the lead site visitor interviewed me for the program director position at his new program, where he served as chairman. After dinner that evening at a fine restaurant, the chairman asked me if I had any questions. I posed only one. "How in the world could you even interview me for this program director position after flagging me with sixteen recommendations at the County?" He smiled and admitted that he was sent to the County with "a job to do." I was simply in a "no-win situation" and I "shouldn't take it personally."

I stayed at the County.

WORKSHOP

In early 1994, I had the privilege of meeting Dr. Robert Marx, a true legend in maxillofacial oncology and reconstruction, at one of his Maxillofacial Soft Tissue Reconstruction cadaver workshops at the University of Miami. It was an eye-opening surgical experience. I invited him to stage such a workshop at Kings County-Downstate Medical Center, and he agreed to come up to Brooklyn in the fall. I was thrilled.

I failed to appreciate how much work I had created for myself. First, I had to procure six fresh cadavers for an anticipated twenty-four participants. Fresh cadavers, not embalmed, were necessary for surgical dissection. They had to be tested for HIV and Hepatitis C. I had to employ the assistance of the anatomy lab staff in the basement of the medical school. The workshop had to be staged before the start of gross anatomy classes in early winter for the first-year medical students. The cadavers had to be stored in freezers until the workshop and then thawed out the night before by the lab techs. I also had to arrange for the cadavers to be disposed of after the workshop. We would require surgical instruments and drills, plus masks, gloves, and gowns too.

All of this came with a hefty price tag. Fortunately, our plating company of choice offered to sponsor the event. Our continuing education department, namely me, had to produce a handsome trifold flier. Then I contacted other OMS training programs in the Greater New York area to ensure full attendance at the workshop for a modest fee. Catering for continental breakfast and lunch had to be arranged as well as ACGME (as a reminder, that stands for Accreditation Council for Graduate Medical Education) continuing education credits.

The highly anticipated Maxillofacial Soft Tissue Reconstruction Workshop at Kings County-SUNY Health Science Center at Brooklyn went off as planned on October 15 and 16. After morning lectures in the medical school auditorium, including mine on anterior and posterior iliac crest bone harvest, we descended on the gross anatomy lab for the cadaver workshop. Mandibular resection, reconstruction plate application, radical neck dissection, and posterior iliac crest bone harvest were all accomplished on the first day. It was carried out under the expert tutelage of Dr. Marx, professor of surgery and chief of OMS at the University of Miami School of Medicine. Dr. Eric Carlson, one of his former fellows who was serving as associate professor of surgery and director of the Center for Maxillofacial Tumor and Reconstructive Surgery, also at Miami, accompanied him.

This workshop would be the start of a career-long academic and social friendship between Eric and me. Our sponsor hosted a dinner for all participants at a great New York steakhouse later that night, after everyone had showered and changed out of their gross anatomy scrubs.

I had arranged for doctors Marx and Carlson to stay at the Battery Park Marriott in downtown New York on Friday and Saturday. When I picked them up early Saturday morning, they recounted a flood, in both their rooms, emanating from a leak in the room above them. As a precaution, they had placed their slide carousels on a table so they wouldn't get ruined. Of course, this was in the days before PowerPoint presentations and USB drives made slides obsolete. In those days, an "expert" was defined as a speaker with more than 100 slides.

Day two of the workshop included pectoralis flaps, abdominal fat harvest, skin grafts, sural nerve harvest, and temporalis flaps. I had arranged for the participants to use the staff locker room in the medical school basement to change before and after the cadaver workshop. Since the medical school was on a skeleton staff that weekend, I didn't anticipate any security problems. On Sunday afternoon after completion of the workshop, I went to change out of my scrubs back into my civilian clothes.

I was dismayed to find my new blue Members Only jacket missing from my locker. Everything else was still there. No other participant noted anything gone. Maybe I had misplaced it.

I drove Marx and Carlson to the airport so they could catch their early evening flight back to Miami. I thanked them profusely. The workshop had been an overwhelming success. Course evaluations were outstanding. But it had been expensive and time consuming. I decided to never again attempt to stage another cadaver workshop without the support of a dedicated continuing education department.

I thought nothing further of my missing jacket until Tuesday, when I met my ENT counterpart for our weekly lunch at the pizza place. Strolling right toward me in a new blue Members Only jacket was a rather large member of the Downstate janitorial staff. The jacket was clearly several sizes too small on him. I diplomatically asked him where he had gotten it. He replied that it had been a gift. I hope he enjoyed it.

FACS

In 1994, I embarked on what would evolve into a rigorous two-year application process to become a Fellow of the American College of Surgeons (FACS). I was already a Diplomate of the American Board of Oral and Maxillofacial Surgery and a Fellow of the American

Association of Oral and Maxillofacial Surgeons—both esteemed organizations with roots in dentistry. At the time, the American College of Surgeons (ACS) was clearly a medical association that required graduation from a fully accredited medical school, completion of at least one year of ACGME accredited residency, and medical licensure.

In fact, back in 1994, it required a dual application process. First as an OMS, I needed five FACS references just to be granted a formal application. That was followed by another five FACS references in the second round. Then I was required to submit my OR log of at least 100 OR cases that I had performed over the previous calendar year. After a torturous two-year journey, I finally found myself seated in the center of a large conference room with more than fifty FACSs staring intently at me. I'm sure they all wondered why an OMS was seeking membership in their college. My interview consisted of only one question, one that I remember to this day: "What is the best lesson you ever learned from a surgical complication?"

Wow. I did a double take. That was like admitting failure, something surgeons rarely discuss. Surprisingly, the answer popped into my head rather quickly. I recounted the case of myositis ossificans traumatica of the masticatory musculature in a lovely, otherwise healthy thirty-year-old Black female. Basically, she had formed heterotopic bone in otherwise normal jaw muscles, preventing her from opening her mouth. I had operated on her on three separate occasions to lyse her bony fusion bilaterally. I even placed interpositional abdominal fat grafts to prevent bone formation. Once, when the reankylosis had fused to the base of her skull, I asked my esteemed head and neck/skull base surgical colleague to join me. Each time, post-op on the OR table, her jaw opening was within normal range (three fingerbreadths).

I even tried multiple adjuvant therapies cited in the orthopedic literature, including high-dose nonsteroidals, steroids, low-dose radiation, bisphosphonates, and physical therapy to minimize heterotopic bone formation. Despite all my efforts, each time, by post-op day fourteen, her jaw opening and function decreased dramatically to less than one fingerbreadth.

Despite these surgical failures, the patient's positive attitude never waned. She was a deeply religious woman who never questioned her fate. On one of her annual follow-up visits, she even brought me a desk set with both our names engraved on it. The best lesson I ever learned from a surgical failure was that not all diseases are amenable to surgery.

~

I guess the interview went well. October 10, 1996, was one of the proudest days of my professional career. My wife and I traveled cross-country to the Moscone Center in San Francisco for my induction as a FACS. I was only the twenty-eighth OMS, at that time, granted Fellowship into the ACS. For me, this journey signified acceptance by my surgical peers and recognition that I was on par with other surgical specialists.

Unfortunately, twenty years later, with the advocacy of AAOMS, the ACS broke precedence and granted a waiver, paving the way for the induction of single-degree OMSs into the college. Totally disconcerted, I wrote a controversial letter to the editor, published in the 2017 edition of the *Journal of Oral and Maxillofacial Surgery* (JOMS). As I ended the letter, "dual-degree OMS FACSs did it the old-fashioned way—we earned it."

RESIDENTS

My early days as program director went relatively smoothly as we expanded the surgical scope of the program while continuing to fulfill accreditation requirements. The personalities of the chief residents set the tone of each year. The actions of certain CRs remain indelibly etched in my memory.

Ninety ninety-five was defined by the single most narcissistic resident in the history of the County. Unbeknownst to me at time, he even took it upon himself to perform post-op physical therapy in the resident on-call room on one of my private fracture patients. I must admit that his altruistic efforts increased the interincisal jaw opening exponentially.

In the mid-1990s, on Fridays after we finished our major OR cases, our service conducted "liver rounds" at the local bar —Kings Corner—across the street from the hospital. Ice cold draft beer, free chips, and excellent brisket sandwiches with fries were all reasonably priced. An eclectic mix of doctors, nurses, and locals from the community favored the fried fish (whiting) sandwiches. Each week, our narcissistic resident would ask the same impatient waitress, "What kind of fish do you have today?" To which she'd reply, "Whitey," eliciting a hearty laugh from our team.

Many of these "liver rounds" were joint affairs with neurosurgery. We took turns recounting our comical patient encounters from the previous week. The cynical and sarcastic NSx chief resident told the tragic tale of a young lady in a coma and his futile attempt to explain the gravity of her situation to the family. "I'm very sorry, but your daughter has an inoperable brain tumor. Her prognosis is grave, and you should make arrangements for the inevitable." Her mother replied, "Lemme get this straight. She has a problem with her main nerve ball?"

Our Friday routine came to an abrupt halt after a midweek late-night shooting incident at the bar, where two Black men in their thirties were shot and killed. Three bullet holes in the walls were visible from the sidewalk. Kings Corner closed down immediately thereafter to be replaced by a law office, specializing in medical malpractice.

⁓

The 1997 and 1999 years were infamous for resident sophomoric behavior. It was hard to believe that a bunch of thirty-year-olds could be so amused by their own flatulence.

One such Asian chief resident was nicknamed "Long Time." This moniker of choice was supposedly indicative of his self-proclaimed sexual prowess. Although in seemingly great shape, he was constantly trying to put on muscle mass. He concocted a breakfast shake that included no less than six raw eggs. He ingested one such shake the morning before our weekly Friday OR session.

Unfortunately for both of us, he was the CR surgeon and I happened to be the OR attending on the very first case of the day. Midway through the case, I was overcome by the foulest of odors emanating from his side of the OR table. He turned a crimson shade of red and started to chuckle. He gleefully admitted ownership of the very flatulence that had somehow permeated through his supposedly impervious OR gown. Even through my surgical mask, my nasal hairs were on fire and my eyes started to tear. Now, I had disimpacted patients while on general surgery, but I had never experienced such a hideous smell. It was as if he had a dead gerbil up his ass. I threw him out of the OR and completed the case with a junior resident.

A second such gaseous misadventure involved another CR taking a facial moulage. This CR was of Irish heritage. His countenance would turn bright red when drinking or laughing. In the late 1990s, we didn't have 3D CT scans or stereolithic models or virtual surgery for our major asymmetry reconstruction cases. Instead, we used dental alginate to take an impression of the entire face. The alginate would serve as a negative. Once poured up in plaster or stone, we would create a lifelike representation of the face. Since the nose and mouth would be covered by the alginate impression material, we would place two nasopharyngeal airways through which the patient would breathe. They were lubricated and passed through both anterior nares prior to the application of the alginate to the face. Somewhat uncomfortable, this required a fair amount of patient cooperation.

One Wednesday p.m. session, I heard a ruckus emanating from the general anesthesia suite. I poked my head in to see a recalcitrant patient lying supine at a thirty-degree angle in the surgical chair. He was undergoing the moulage procedure prior to planned reconstruction of his facial asymmetry. He was breathing heavily through the requisite two nasopharyngeal airways exiting his nostrils like elephant tusks. The alginate covered his eyes, nose, and mouth.

The CR became somewhat disconcerted by the lack of patient cooperation. As the alginate set in place, the CR turned and must have passed gas. It was silent but almost deadly, as the patient inhaled the fumes through the nasal trumpets. He started to thrash around in utter disgust. The CR's face turned scarlet red as he left the operatory, laughing hysterically. The junior resident peeled the alginate impression from the patient's face. The impression was perfect. The patient did not have a seizure. But once again, I had to chastise another CR for his unwarranted juvenile, unprofessional behavior.

Nineteen ninety-eight was infamous for the behavior of one of our CRs at the AAOMS Annual Meeting in Miami. Evidently, he had a bit too much to drink the night of the President's Gala and passed out on South Beach. He awakened to realize that in his drunken stupor he had been rolled. His watch and wallet were stolen. He was too embarrassed to report it to the police.

Nineteen ninety-nine was best remembered as the "wonderful world of airway," a term coined by my longtime ENT friend and fellow program director, Dr. Gady Har-El, a renowned head and neck colleague. He remains one of the bravest surgeons I've ever scrubbed in with. Up to this point, I had served as attending on all emergency tracheostomies for our major orofacial infection patients. I had previously performed numerous trachs while rotating on the neurosurgery service and as a general surgery resident. Doing an elective trach over a secured intubated airway on a ventilator-dependent patient is a nonstressful procedure. Performing an emergency trach on a patient with a tenuous airway, and a neck like the Michelin man, is quite a different story. It is certainly not the simple, safe procedure portrayed in television medical dramas. I had puckered my way through several emergency trachs when anesthesia couldn't intubate the patient, even fiberoptically, and lost the airway. Most of my on-call attendings didn't feel comfortable with the procedure.

But, I couldn't be on-call every night of the year. So, my ENT counterpart and I established an airway protocol to minimize the number of anesthesia airway misadventures and resultant slash trachs by our surgical teams. Although I felt strongly that OMS residents needed to be trained to perform elective tracheostomies, I was well aware that our ENT colleagues were far more adept and faster at emergency trachs than we were.

So, based on our clinical assessment of the patient, a fiberoptic exam of the airway, and a CT scan if the patient was stable enough to tolerate it, we would reach a joint assessment about whether the patient could be safely intubated. If we determined the airway to be patent, ENT would be on standby while anesthesia attempted to fiber-optically intubate the patient. If intubation seemed dubious at best, then ENT would perform a controlled trach under local anesthesia before the airway was lost. Hopefully, this would obviate the need for the dreaded slash trach with its impending complications. Usually an ENT CR, who had performed hundreds of trachs during his or her residency, would take one of my CRs through the procedure. A trach for an ENT CR was comparable to an impacted wisdom tooth extraction for one of my CRs. If the ENT attending was unavailable on short notice, then I would cover the case. This protocol was based on a collegial relationship between both services. More importantly, it saved me from much wear and tear on my cardiovascular system.

Over the next twenty years at the County, our joint airway protocol worked remarkably well. We even published it and presented it at a poster session at one of our Annual AAOMS Meetings. However, there was one notable exception. Early on in 1999, our CR, an ENT senior resident, and a young anesthesia attending violated the estab-lished protocol. Sensing an imminent loss of airway due to a Ludwig's angina, or severe bilateral cervicofacial infection, they rushed a young Black male to the OR. Anesthesia couldn't fiberoptically intubate the patient and lost the airway. Attempts to perform an emergency tracheostomy were complicated by a previous gunshot wound to the superior mediastinum, displacing the innominate artery into the field. This major vessel was injured during the rushed dissection down to the trachea, which caused a major arterial bleed.

Fortunately, the cardiothoracic surgery fellow was scrubbed in on a chest trauma case in the OR directly across the hall. He performed an emergent sternotomy to gain control of the innominate artery as it came off the aortic arch. Together, with the OMS and ENT residents, they completed the trach. The associate OMS director, who had the misfortune to be on-call that night, finally arrived and entered the room. To his utter dismay, he saw a patient with his chest cracked open and blood all over the floor. Thinking it must be a cardiothoracic surgery case, he declared, "Sorry, wrong room." Before he could exit, the OR nurses advised him that it was, in fact, his OMS patient. "WTF!" he exclaimed.

Amazingly, the patient survived with minimal complications except, of course, for that long sternal incision, which earned him a sizable malpractice settlement. This violation of airway protocol caused me to rip my CR a new asshole.

Later that year, we set another record that still stands. One spring afternoon, EMS brought in a tall, slim thirty-year-old Black male to the C-1 acute trauma unit. He was unconscious, intubated in the field, with a cervical collar in place. Evidently, he was a six-story jumper from the balcony of a local high-rise apartment. Six stories is usually the cut-off for patient survival. Nevertheless, after aggressive resuscitation, he was reasonably stable. Full body CT scans revealed bilateral lower extremity, pelvic, and right wrist fractures. Neurosurgery and ophthalmology were consulted; there was no evidence of intracranial bleed or shift nor ruptured globe. The OMS service was consulted for panfacial fractures.

The orthopedic surgery team rushed him to the OR to reduce and stabilize his extensive compound fractures. The OMS team followed once Anesthesia deemed him stable enough to continue the lengthy operation. After we converted his oral intubation to a formal trach, we proceeded to perform ORIFs (again, that's open reduction and internal fixation) of his tri-mandible and LeFort III fractures. Via a bicoronal flap, we obliterated his frontal sinus fracture and performed ORIFs of multiple frontal fractures. After fourteen hours of two-team surgery and six units of blood products, he was transported to the SICU in surprisingly stable condition.

It was now sunrise. Time for our favorite local bakery, Master Lou's, to open for the day. An extra-large coffee and a Caribbean Delight pastry provided the carb surge I needed to get my second wind. The OMS team returned to the SICU to make post-op rounds on the patient. He was starting to regain consciousness. Much to our collective surprise, he was shackled to the bed with handcuffs to his left wrist—the only remaining extremity not in a cast. We had all foolishly assumed his injuries were the result of a failed suicide attempt. Upon further police investigation at the scene, it turned out that he had jumped off the balcony of the sixth floor apartment he was burglarizing when the gun-wielding tenant arrived home unexpectedly in the middle of the afternoon. Yes, we had all been a bit too presumptive.

A great case, a good post-op result, a good lesson for us all, and our plating company was ecstatic. All told, the OMS team had placed a record ninety-six plates and screws to reduce and fixate his panfacial fractures. His post-op radiographs looked like an erector set.

～

In the early days of my directorship, typically our primary plating company sponsored a graduation dinner/workshop in June and a holiday dinner/workshop in December for our OMS residents and attendings. These events occurred at one of our favorite New York City steakhouses. I remained brand loyal to one plating company at a time. It was a symbiotic relationship: We used almost half a million dollars of their hardware per year, and they provided a good product backed by timely, responsive service. If it was left up to the residents, however, they would have whored themselves out to one company for breakfast, a second company for lunch, and a third for dinner. It must be pointed out that by the turn of the century, corporate compliance regulations on both sides prohibited such interactions.

Peter Luger Steak House is universally acknowledged as the best steakhouse in the country. It was established in 1887 in the shadow of the Williamsburg Bridge, a century before the Brooklyn neighborhood became gentrified. In fact, back in the 1990s, we literally had an armed guard escort us from their parking lot, next to the old bank across the street, to the restaurant. Zagat has even rated it the number one steakhouse in New York City for thirty consecutive years. Too bad, because of one harrowing episode, I will never step foot in that restaurant again.

We had scheduled our annual graduation dinner at Peter Luger one Wednesday night in June. The restaurant had only two seatings for large parties over twenty-five people, at four thirty and eight, and they didn't take credit cards, only cash or their own Peter Luger card. Our plating company rep made the reservation for the early seating figuring we would get out of clinic by four thirty, shoot down Bedford Avenue to Broadway, and arrive by five. Some of our private attendings wouldn't meander in till six. The rep put the $500 deposit to hold the table on his newly minted Peter Luger card. No problem, or so we thought. The maître d' refused to seat us at five until our entire party arrived. So, we proceeded to tote up a $500 bar tab. By six, the rep notified the maître d' that everyone had arrived and we were ready to be seated. The maître d' smugly informed us that since we weren't ready to be seated at five he had given our table away. We assured him that we'd be done with dinner by his next seating at eight. Too late, done deal. Disappointed, but still somewhat civil, we made a last-minute reservation at one of our go-to Italian restaurants on the waterfront that was more than happy to accommodate our large party.

It was now time to settle the bar tab. That's when the shit hit the fan. Our rep told the bartender to take the bar bill off the $500 deposit he had left on his Peter Luger card. No dice. The maître d' told him the deposit was forfeited and he had to settle the bar bill on top of it. Now the rep's regional manager, who had to authorize all expenditures over $500, got involved. He was a good guy, but at an athletic six foot six, he was an imposing figure with boxing experience. By now, his neck was turning a scarlet shade of red. Suddenly, a five-by-five bouncer, seemingly right out of the newly released *Sopranos* on HBO, appeared. He suggested our entire group take it outside. It was getting ugly really fast. Somehow, I calmed down the regional manager, who begrudgingly paid the bar bill. We mobilized and reconvened at our second-choice Italian restaurant.

The next day, the Peter Luger manager evidently called our rep and offered to refund the $500 on his Luger card. He told her to shove it up her ass. As for me, I never stepped foot in Peter Luger Steak House again. Several of Luger's headwaiters have splintered off over the years and opened their own steakhouses in New York City and elsewhere. That includes my favorites, Wolfgang's in New York City and Andre's in Naples.

INDIA TRIP – FIVE STAR

The year 2000 was unique. Firstly, due to attrition, I was down to only one chief resident. Secondly, I was invited to join two outstanding surgeons, Eric Carlson, DMD, MD, FACS and Ghali Ghali, DDS, MD, FACS on a head and neck cancer trip to India sponsored by Health Volunteers Overseas in January. At the time, Dr. Carlson was professor and chairman at the University of Tennessee, Knoxville, while Dr. Ghali served as professor and chairman at Louisiana State University, Shreveport. We were to be accompanied by a colleague from the Pacific Northwest and my CR, who had lobbied vociferously to join me. Now, I had already gone on several safari surgery cleft lip and palate trips to Mexico, but this would be special.

For starters, I needed a visa to enter India for this seventeen-day sojourn as a lecturer and surgeon. Secondly, I needed multiple vaccinations four to six weeks in advance besides the standard vaccinations I had already received. This included Hepatitis A, typhoid fever, and meningococcal vaccines. Besides Cipro (ciprofloxacin) for traveler's diarrhea, there was the issue of taking a prophylactic antimalarial. In 2000, Lariam (mefloquine) was the CDC-recommended malaria prophylaxis of choice. The US Army had developed it in the 1970s, and it came into widespread usage in the 1980s. But, it had a well-documented neuro-psychiatric profile of causing depression, hallucinations, insomnia, and anxiety. By 2013, the US Army banned its usage. Currently, Malarone (atovaquone plus proguanil) is the drug of choice. Unfortunately for me, I fell into the 13.5 percent of Lariam users who experience insomnia, which I endured for my entire trip to India.

Our trip was split into two components, including an academic leg in Chandigarh followed by the surgical leg in Jabalpur. Team members flew from their respective cities to Amsterdam, where we met up in the Amsterdam airport for our connecting flight to New Delhi. Turned out that the New Delhi airport was fogged in, evidently a fairly common occurrence, and we were delayed until morning.

The Amsterdam airport was quite modern and remarkably clean. I scrambled to find the very last available room in the only terminal hotel that wouldn't require another trip through customs. My CR and I shared a double bed; no twin beds were available, so we had to make do with a strict no-spooning rule. By morning, our flight took off at its rescheduled departure time. The eight-hour flight to New Delhi was fine, except for the still dense fog that necessitated an instrument landing. We cleared customs and were instantly overwhelmed by the smell of gasoline and burnt rubber as we exited the terminal. The air quality was so poor that I immediately vowed to stop smoking cigars or my pipe for the duration of the trip. That's when the adventure to Chandigarh started.

Chandigarh was India's first planned city, with a population of more than one million. It was the dream city of India's first prime minister, Jawaharlal Nehru. Located in northern India, it is the capital of both the Punjabi and Hindi speaking state of Haryana and is billed as the modern academic and medical center of the country. Chandigarh is 260 kilometers (160 miles) north of New Delhi, a four-hour train ride on the Shatabdi Express.

We had missed our train the day before, and it was now booked solid. Our host OMS scrambled to find two "limo" drivers for the supposed five-hour ride north. We split into two cars. The two stars were in the nicer car; my CR, my colleague from Seattle, and I were in the second car. Now, these limos weren't exactly Lincoln Town Cars. Little did I know that we got into the wrong car.

It is evidently quite acceptable to travel by car on National Highway 1 from New Delhi to Chandigarh in spring, summer, and fall. Unbeknownst to our travel party, it should be avoided in the winter months due to heavy fog. We departed midafternoon under clear skies. We hadn't driven fifty kilometers before our first tire blew out. No problem. Our driver hastily changed it, swapping in the bald spare he had in the trunk. While he was changing the tire with my chief resident's assistance, I quickly noted that the three other tires were equally bald. I asked the driver if we should stop somewhere and buy another spare; he agreed. We had barely made it another fifty kilometers when another tire blew out. Fortunately, we had the recently purchased second spare to replace it. Miraculously, we made it another 100 kilometers before the third tire blew out. We rolled into a nearby petrol station that gladly changed the tire for us. Unfortunately, they had only one tire suitable for our car. We were just sixty kilometers from Chandigarh, so we decided to take a chance to try to get there without a fourth spare.

Now, it was getting dark and starting to rain. Sure enough, twenty kilometers south of Chandigarh, the fourth bald tire blew out. The international cell phone service I had purchased didn't work. My CR and I walked to the nearest petrol station, which turned out to be only one kilometer north. By now, the bilingual Hindi/English signs had changed to Hindi/Punjabi. At the petrol station, no one spoke English. The petrol attendant started to converse with my CR. He was somewhat taken back when he realized that my Indian CR didn't speak a word of Hindi. My CR was actually American born of Mormon descent and had played football at Utah State. Built like the running back he was in college, he liked to hunt buffalo and fish in Utah. The petrol attendant managed to convey the fact that he had no tires to purchase. He was kind enough to let us use his phone, but there was no reception.

We were stuck in the deserted absolute middle of nowhere with no connection to civilization. We walked back to the car to wait with the others until our colleagues in the other car would hopefully become aware of our absence and send a search party back for us. Two hours passed before the hotel courtesy car spotted us. Fortunately, he had a brand-new spare tire.

We hopped back into the car for the final leg of our journey. Now, the fog was so dense that we couldn't see ten feet in front of us. It was also raining briskly, and the windshield wipers only worked intermittently. These facts didn't slow down our driver. As we approached the outskirts of Chandigarh, he persisted, over my objections, to pass old, rickety double-decker buses along the single-lane road.

Miraculously, we arrived at our hotel in Chandigarh by midnight. I was pissed off, but our colleagues, who had arrived four hours earlier, found our misadventure somewhat amusing. Not so funny! The next day, I read in an English Chandigarh newspaper that two Americans, days earlier, had been mugged along the very same highway we had traveled. It was a good thing my CR was built like a bull.

For the first leg of our trip, we stayed in the newest hotel in Chandigarh. It was modern, clean, and had running water, supplying a shower and a toilet that flushed. The hotel food was safe to eat and quite good Indian fare. The bar was well stocked with top-shelf alcohol. Unfortunately, there was a Hindu wedding going on for the requisite five nights during our stay. The nightly noise emanating from the atrium made sleeping almost impossible. The first night upon my arrival, I called the desk and requested a bottle of water. Moments later, the bellhop knocked on the door with a two-liter Beefeater bottled water. I handed him a fifty rupee ($1) tip for his efforts. He thanked me profusely. Two minutes later, the hotel manager arrived at my door with the bellhop in tow and asked me if he had stolen the money. I assured the manager that the bellhop had not. Evidently, a ten rupee tip or twenty cent tip would have been more appropriate.

The Chandigarh leg of the trip was productive. All four Americans each gave a "keynote" lecture to the Indian Association of OMS (IAOMS) at a modern conference center. The IAOMS was a great host, big on pomp and circumstance. It awarded each of us a handsome plaque and beautiful flowers. Of course, the power went out in the middle of my hour-long "Mandible Fracture Protocol-2000" lecture. None of the 1,000 people in the audience seemed the least surprised by this temporary inconvenience. The Lariam-fueled insomnia finally got to me, as I almost fell asleep while judging the poster session. I selected an excellent poster on "Treatment of Submucous Fibrosis," which is prevalent in India due to the rampant chewing of betel nuts.

One night, I needed a break from the Indian food in the hotel, so I called the local Pizza Hut, which gladly delivered. After just one bite, I realized that they used goat cheese rather than mozzarella. Forget that idea; I gave the rest of the pie to the bellhop.

No trip to Chandigarh is complete without a visit to the Rock Garden, which a humble transport officer named Nek Chand Saini designed more than sixty years ago. He used recyclable ceramics from industrial and home waste, even toilets, for his truly remarkable sculptures.

After a week, we progressed to the second leg of our trip in Jabalpur. Jabalpur, located in the center of India, has a population of more than one million. To travel there, we had to first take the four-hour train ride we had initially missed back to New Delhi. We arrived in New Delhi with a few hours to kill. Our host suggested we go to the nearby five-star Radisson Hotel for lunch. The buffet food at the Radisson was imported from England, so it was expensive but worth every penny. I was in ecstasy. That's when my colleagues first gave me the nickname "Five Star." I guess I had proven that I wasn't a good third world traveler.

After cleaning up in the seemingly palatial hotel restroom, we had a short cab ride to the railway station, a veritable TB incubator with hundreds of people packed in, coughing and smoking nonstop. Thankfully, our train pulled in on time. Our host whisked me and my two friends to our first-class cabin for the seventeen-hour train ride to Jabalpur. Although hardly up to US first-class standards, it was serviceable except for two minor points. First, our host advised us to lock our suitcases to the seats as thieves were known to move through the cars at night. Second, the first-class bathroom was actually a hole in the floor between train cars. We were directed not to use the facilities during scheduled stops. The night passed uneventfully as my friends and I shared war stories from our training days.

When we pulled into Jabalpur, it was nighttime. I forgot we had chosen to come to India in January to avoid the subtropical climate in the spring and summer and the southwest monsoon season in early fall. When we disembarked from the train, it was a cool forty-five degrees Fahrenheit. Our host arranged cabs to the local hotel, which he happened to own. It was located near the hospital—which he also owned—which was located directly across the street from the local leprosy hospital, which he didn't own.

The hotel was the most expensive in town at $7 per night. We were advised to cover our mouths while showering and, of course, to brush our teeth with bottled water. The urinal was a hole in the bathroom floor, and the toilet flushed occasionally, though only if you were lucky. Our host just happened to also own the local restaurant, which catered to our needs. We were instructed not to eat anything that was not thoroughly cooked or peeled. I lived on chicken tikka (chicken on a skewer charbroiled in a tandoor), saffron rice, and naan bread. Our Seattle colleague was a bit more adventurous. On return from a trip to the Marble Rocks, a beautiful gorge along the Narmada River, we stopped for a quick snack at an outdoor café. I just ordered a bottle of soda, but he insisted on trying the local salad. He spent the next two days in his hotel room hooked up to an IV.

We were quite busy the entire week in Jabalpur. Our host OMS had scheduled a plethora of head and neck cancer cases for our team every day. We broke into three teams and operated nonstop due to the high local incidence of head and neck cancer. In India, head and neck cases represent 30 to 40 percent of all reported cancers. Roughly 20 percent of all new head and neck cancers in the world are diagnosed there. This is due to multiple socioeconomic and ethnic practices, including tobacco usage, chewing betel nuts, alcohol consumption, and environmental carcinogens.

Our host set up a closed-circuit camera in one operatory and telecasted the surgeries to local OMS, ENT, and general surgeons gathered in his conference room. In just one day, I scrubbed in with my LSU colleague, who displayed his broad diversity of expertise by performing a radical neck dissection and tongue flap for a floor-of-mouth squamous cell carcinoma, a LeFort I osteotomy for vertical maxillary excess, and a cleft lip repair on a baby. Our team performed a parotidectomy, a thyroidectomy, resections of TMJ ankylosis (seen commonly in India in kids thrown off bicycle handlebars), and mandibular resections. The level of general anesthesia care was outstanding despite the minimal technology. The post-op care was more than adequate, with family members often sleeping in the ward next to the patients. Although I had not been a big fan of safari surgery due to the lack of post-op care during my prior experiences, our host assured us that the local surgeons observing our cases would provide all necessary follow-up.

The patients and their families were incredibly appreciative. Our host and his family were more than friendly and supportive. But, I'll never forget the sign for a local cybercafé that was located right next to a drainage ditch with sewage flowing downhill. It was a shocking juxtaposition of high technology, with an abundance of cellphones and laptops, paired with a stark lack of infrastructure. Unfortunately, Jabalpur remains a third world city.

After a week in Jabalpur, we bade our host adieu and took the train back to New Delhi to catch our returning flight to Amsterdam and onto the US. On the way back, we stopped in Agra to see the Taj Mahal. One of the Seven Wonders of the World, the Taj Mahal is an ivory-white domed marble mausoleum, commissioned in 1632 by the Mughal emperor Shah Jahan to house the tomb of his favorite wife, Mumtaz Mahal. It also houses the tomb of Shah Jahan himself. In 1653, it was completed at an estimated cost of about thirty-two million rupees, which would equate to roughly one billion US dollars today. It was truly a spectacular sight. Unfortunately, we arrived in Agra on a Monday and found the Taj Mahal was closed to visitors. Although disappointed, we hired a guide, who shepherded us around the grounds. His makeshift tour was briefly interrupted by a herd of rather emaciated cattle that sauntered past us.

Before heading back to the train to New Delhi, we stopped at the Agra Pizza Hut. Thank goodness for the eight million visitors to the Taj each year. This Pizza Hut served real pizza baked with mozzarella cheese. I wolfed down a whole pie myself.

Our train pulled into New Delhi just in time to catch a cab to the airport. Our team flew west back to Amsterdam, except for our adventurous colleague who flew east over the Pole back to Seattle. In the Amsterdam airport, our team said its goodbyes and split up for our respective flights back to the US. I flew into Newark airport and landed in a snowstorm. Evidently, the airport prioritizes the international flights when it keeps one runway open. I coasted through customs, happy to be back on US soil. I was lucky to flag down a cabdriver who drove me home through the blinding snow. For a generous tip, he helped me carry my suitcases and assorted India memorabilia up the unplowed driveway.

It had been a successful trip. We gave lectures, treated patients, made some new friends, and experienced India. I learned that I'm not a good third world traveler, lost seventeen pounds, and earned the nickname "5 Star."

Director II: 2001–2010

TRIPLE THREAT

The year 2001 was the most stressful year to date because of constantly pushing the surgical envelope. That year, we were back to our three allotted chief residents. Each of the three CRs was equally aggressive in bringing cases to the OR. In fact, they each tried to outdo the other two. It was not uncommon to be in the OR until midnight on Friday nights because each CR scheduled a long case on the same day.

Each CR had his own surgical area of interest, namely oncology, cosmetic surgery, or orthognathic surgery. Each made a concerted effort to push our surgical scope in that particular area. The charge of the program director, as I saw it, was to expand the surgical envelope based on proper training, credentials, and expertise. However, my responsibility was also primarily to our patients. This meant to provide the very best care while remembering our Hippocratic Oath to "first do no harm."

So, before performing the first parotidectomy in the history of the OMS service at Kings County, I had made sure to arrange a visit with Dr. Robert Marx at the University of Miami-Jackson Memorial Hospital. He was gracious enough to invite me to present my "Mandible Fracture Protocol" lecture to his department. While there I observed several parotid surgeries. Upon return to the County, I scrubbed in with my ENT counterpart on a few parotids. To avoid any potential turf wars, I agreed to limit our parotid surgery to tumors confirmed as benign or inflammatory on fine needle aspiration (FNA), such as pleomorphic adenomas. I have no doubt my medical degree and medical license greased the wheels of the Credentials Committee in getting this privilege approved.

We performed that first parotidectomy without complication. Yes, we even had a few general surgery and ENT colleagues stop into our OR to check out what the "dentists" were up to now. Identification of the root of the seventh cranial nerve was a bit time consuming, and skeletonization of the five branches of the facial nerve was a bit tedious. We completed the superficial parotidectomy, and it was an elegant dissection indeed. Frozen section confirmed the benign diagnosis of pleomorphic adenoma; margins were clear.

While awaiting the histopathologic diagnosis, we harvested a fat graft via a modified Pfannenstiel incision in the lower abdomen. Placing this graft into the parotid defect would serve two purposes: It would ameliorate any cosmetic defect, and it would help prevent Frey's Syndrome, or gustatory sweating, a reported complication after parotid surgery due to injury to the auriculotemporal nerve. Simply put, it involves crossover of parasympathetic salivation fibers to the parotid gland with sympathetic fibers to the sweat glands. Patients who develop this unfortunate complication will have facial sweating when chewing. Post-op, the patient did well with no evidence of facial nerve deficit.

We also performed the first rhinoplasties in the history of the OMS service at the County, in 2001. Rather than take a weekend matchbook course on rhinoplasty, I arranged to scrub in on multiple rhinoplasties with my ENT and plastic surgery colleagues. Although initially suspicious of my motives, they welcomed me when I assured them we would only tackle post-traumatic (nasal fractures) or post-orthognathic rhinoplasties. We started with simple endonasal rhinoplasties such as dorsal hump reductions and Weir alar base reductions. Eventually, the CRs pushed the envelope to include calvaria bone grafts for saddle deformities, septoplasties, and dome modification via an open rhinoplasty exposure. One of our former OMS residents who had gone on to plastics at the County joined us in the OR to share his newfound expertise. But no, we never recruited Little Janie from suburbia for a totally elective rhinoplasty.

It came as no surprise that the three chief residents from the Class of 2001 became the most accomplished group I ever trained in terms of obtaining prestigious fellowships. One became the first of four County OMS residents over the next seventeen years to complete two years of head and neck oncology and microvascular reconstruction with Dr. Robert Ord, professor and chairman at the University of Maryland. I assume Dr. Ord found our residents to be well trained and ready to hit the ground running. He didn't have to reinvent the wheel with our graduates.

A second 2001 CR went on to complete a requisite second year of general surgery before pursuing two years of plastic and reconstructive surgery at Wayne State in Detroit. This was followed by a year of Craniofacial Surgery Fellowship at Stanford. The third 2001 CR was an orthognathic surgery machine during his chief year at the County. He almost satisfied our thirty-case requirement by himself. He also pushed for our participation in the new field of distraction osteogenesis. He even earned his own recovery room overnight observation bed due to his high rate of post-op iatrogenic epistaxis cases. After completing his four-year OMS certificate residency, he elected to go back to Downstate Medical College, with advanced standing into their third-year class. He then completed a year of general surgery at Downstate for medical licensure. Subsequently, he completed a year of Cosmetic Surgery Fellowship in Columbus, Ohio.

Yes, all three 2001 chief residents had pushed the envelope and expanded the scope of the OMS department. It had been a constant battle for me to control the reins, but it was worth it in the end.

9/11

September 11, 2001, will live on in infamy. Due to Kings County's proximity to the World Trade Center, we had a bird's-eye view of the deadliest attack on US soil. Every American who lived through it will never forget where they were and what they were doing that Tuesday morning.

I was looking, as I usually did, at the Twin Towers as I drove over the Verrazano Bridge into Brooklyn. It was a beautiful, crystal-blue, cloudless late summer sky. Visibility was impeccable; I could see for miles in all directions. I finished my seven a.m. physical diagnosis lecture to the residents. I had just strolled into our administrative assistant's office at eight thirty a.m. to sign in on those somewhat degrading time sheets. Within minutes, I overheard an emergency news flash coming from the radio that a plane had just flown into the World Trade Center. We all rushed back into our E building ground floor department conference room and turned on the television to check it out. I assumed it must have been a small private plane that had wandered off course. We were all aghast to find out that it was, in fact, a commercial jetliner. American Airlines Flight 11, a Boeing 767 aircraft, had departed Logan airport in Boston at 7:59 a.m. en route to Los Angeles with a crew of eleven, seventy-six passengers, and the five hijackers. It crashed into the northern façade of the North Tower of the World Trade Center at 8:46 a.m. This was no accident; it was clearly an act of terrorism.

Several of us ran to the B building, still the second tallest structure in Brooklyn after the Williamsburgh Savings Bank. As I ran through a parking lot where I always parked, I came across one of my former general surgery attendings. He was walking to his clinic in the E building and was unaware of the catastrophe that had just unfolded. I notified him of the attack; he turned around and joined us. We took the crowded elevator to the eleventh floor of the B building and climbed the narrow stairs to the fenced-in roof. We looked northwest at the smoke billowing from the North Tower, less than ten miles away. Suddenly, we saw a second plane crash into the southern façade of the South Tower of the World Trade Center at 9:03 a.m. It turned out to be United Airlines Flight 175, another Boeing 767 aircraft, that had departed Logan airport at 8:14 a.m. with a crew of nine, fifty-one passengers, and five hijackers. We couldn't believe our eyes when the South Tower collapsed at 9:59 a.m. due to fire-induced structural failure. The North Tower collapsed at 10:28 a.m. We later learned that another group of five hijackers had flown American Airlines Flight 77 into the Pentagon at 9:37 a.m. United Airlines Flight 93 had crashed in a field in Shanksville, Pennsylvania, at 10:03 a.m. as its passengers attempted to subdue four hijackers.

As the primary New York City Health and Hospitals Corporation disaster hospital for all of Brooklyn, we anticipated mass casualties. I rushed down to the B building first-floor boardroom, where the command center was hastily set up. Our department's roles were twofold. The dental clinic was to be a triage center where our junior residents would suture minor lacerations. The chief of the trauma service designated OMS responsible for surgical airways, as tracheostomies were anticipated for airway compromise induced by severe smoke inhalation. Yes, OMS had come a long way indeed.

I took my CRs and seniors who were on the service to the C-1 acute trauma ER. There we awaited the first casualties to arrive. We waited, and waited, and waited some more. One of my colleagues from the India trip still swears to this day that he saw me on TV in my white coat and scrubs standing outside the C building trauma entrance. Unfortunately, there were very few survivors of the attack. The only patient I saw that day was a stunned, incoherent, ash-covered middle-aged Black man who had apparently walked over the Brooklyn Bridge and continued five miles to the County. He had only minor smoke inhalation and didn't require intubation or tracheostomy.

As soon as the first plane crashed into the North Tower, I tried to reach my wife. However, cellphones were down, and landlines were swamped. Eventually, I reached Helaine at 9:30 a.m. She had been playing tennis with her girlfriend and was totally oblivious to what had transpired. At this point, no one knew if these were four isolated attacks or if we were at war. Helaine ran to the schools and picked up our three kids. Not until midnight did the County's command center release the disaster team to go home.

Ultimately, the coordinated terrorist attacks resulted in 2,977 fatalities and upwards of 25,000 injuries. First responders suffered severe losses: seventy-three law enforcement officers and 343 firefighters were killed. We later learned that the 9/11 jihad was the work of the Islamic terrorist group al-Qaeda. It was orchestrated by Osama bin Laden and masterminded by Khalid Sheikh Mohammed. Thousands of rescue workers eventually developed fatal or long-term debilitating illnesses due to the toxic debris at Ground Zero.

President George W. Bush's popularity soared after the attacks. In 2003, he launched his ill-conceived Iraq War to overthrow Saddam Hussein and eliminate his weapons of mass destruction (which never existed). Rudy Giuliani became known as America's Mayor for his mayoral leadership during and after the attack. Fifteen years later, he would lose all credibility after becoming President Donald Trump's personal attorney and attack dog.

As for me, my commute became sheer torture for the next few months after 9/11. One lane in each direction on the Staten Island Expressway was closed off to routine traffic. This allowed quick passage of dump trucks carrying rubble from Ground Zero to the Fresh Kills Landfill in Staten Island. There, forensic specialists attempted to recover human remains from the debris. One day while stuck in bumper-to-bumper traffic heading east on the Expressway, I couldn't take it anymore. I had an eight a.m. case at Brookdale Medical Center, one of our affiliates. It was already seven thirty a.m., and I had been on the road since five. I jumped into the restricted lane and was soon stopped by police at a checkpoint. I explained my plight to the officer, who was gracious enough to provide me with a police escort over the Verrazano Bridge. He also told me not to dare try that ever again.

HOPSCOTCH

From 2000 to 2006, I actively sought out chairman or chief positions as they became available. With only 108 OMS programs in the country, these positions were highly competitive with rare turnover.

But by 2000, I was feeling quite restricted in my position as program director at the County. Unlike others who aspired to ascend the academic ladder, I didn't have a mentor as chairman to support me but rather an outsider in the OMS community.

Over this six-year period, I was offered three chair positions at fine institutions. First, there was the chief of the OMS division in the surgery department at Henry Ford Hospital in Detroit. I flew into Detroit from Newark airport on three separate occasions for a series of interviews with everyone, from OMS attendings, ENT and plastics chiefs, the chairman of surgery, and the hospital CEO.

I got to learn firsthand why Northwest Airlines was nicknamed NorthWorst. Once, Northwest called me at midnight to inform me that my six a.m. flight the following morning had been canceled, so they were holding a seat for me on their eight a.m. flight. I suspect the CEO wasn't too impressed when I showed up at eleven a.m. for a nine a.m. meeting. Nonetheless, the chairman of surgery offered me the position at a significant pay raise from my salary at Kings County. He was, in fact, a regent on the board of the American College of Surgeons and was quite impressed with my FACS status. He flew my wife and me out to Detroit for my third set of interviews. Afterward, we went to dinner at a fine restaurant in Bloomfield Hills, an upscale suburb twenty miles north of Detroit.

I excitedly signed the contract. I was due to start after Labor Day in 2000. I gave my three months' notice at the County; my chairman was less than supportive. I even wrote the "faculty position available" ad in the AAOMS classifieds to recruit my successor. I put my house in Marlboro, New Jersey, on the market. In late June, I put the entire family in the car for a road trip to go house hunting in beautiful Detroit. Henry Ford Hospital hooked me up with a real estate agent who handled their faculty relocations. For three days, we hunted in the northwest suburbs of Detroit. We settled on a lovely house that Helaine liked, on the fifth hole of a golf course in Farmington Hills off 12 Mile Road.

Everything was progressing well. We even had a buyer for our house. Then all hell broke loose that August. First, I was diagnosed with skin cancer of my neck. It was only a basal cell carcinoma, so I thought it was no big deal. I was wrong as it turned out to be of the Morpheus subtype. That meant it was more infiltrative and tended to extend subcutaneously beyond its clinically delineated borders. After three separate wide excisions, the last including frozen sections in the OR, my margins were finally clear. Perhaps Mohs micrographic surgery would have been a wiser choice. I guess all those summers at the beach in my younger years using Hawaiian Tropic Tanning Oil might have been foolhardy after all.

Then my mother, seventy-four, sustained three vertebral compression fractures of her lumbar spine. This was excruciatingly painful for both of us. I had her admitted to Rusk Institute at New York University for rehab and pain control. The worst idea my sister ever had was to give her a cellphone with my number on speed dial. Totally disoriented on Oxycontin, my mother would call me at all hours of the night from her hospital bed. She was oriented enough, however, to play the guilt card regarding my decision to leave her to go to Detroit.

Right around this time, my chairman stepped up to the plate and made me an offer I couldn't refuse. He told the CEO at the County that he wasn't satisfied with the candidates for my replacement. They agreed to essentially juggle pay lines to double my salary and promote me to director of service, which would make me management. He arranged with the medical school to fast-track my promotion to associate professor of surgery. It seems the administration never appreciates you until you threaten to leave. Now in all honesty, I hadn't placed a down payment on a house outside of Detroit, accepted a down payment on my house in New Jersey, and signed a contract for leverage. I freaked out. It was *not* my finest moment. Sheepishly, I called the head of the Henry Ford search committee, who begrudgingly released me from my contract. I lost my down payment in Farmington Hills; I paid the real estate agent for his efforts. Needless to say, my real estate agent in New Jersey wasn't too happy with me.

It is always easier to stay than uproot your family to move across the country. But, as I've since learned the hard way, you must be willing to jump around the country if you're going to ascend the academic ladder.

Four years later, in 2004, Mount Sinai Hospital in New York City had an open chairman position. This time, an ENT surgeon on their staff who knew me through a mutual colleague recruited me. Their highly respected OMS chairman was leaving to join his head and neck microvascular surgical colleague at Beth Israel downtown. Again, I went through a rigorous three-stage interview process, including with the dean of the Mount Sinai Medical School and the hospital president. They assigned me a practice planner who was only interested in how many private patients I could bring with me as well as how many new patients I could attract to the medical center. Ultimately, they offered me the position at a generous salary but with an interesting "sundown" clause. Each year, my guaranteed salary would decrease proportionately while my faculty practice was expected to grow based on Mount Sinai's reputation. Although I had my reservations, the good news was that I wouldn't have to move and disrupt my family. I accepted the position.

A full welcome reception was scheduled for me on a winter Friday. With an impending snowstorm, Mount Sinai offered to put me up in one of their boutique hotels on Madison Avenue. The room was tiny, but at least I beat the storm. Friday morning, unable to get a cab in the snow, I trudged the ten blocks to the hospital with my four slide carousels in tow (still no PowerPoint in those days) for my eight a.m. lecture. I met with the attending staff, residents, and support staff. Previously unbeknownst to me, they had been promoting my arrival to their prospective applicants at their interviews. Turns out the director of general dentistry had contacted my chairman at the County to do a background check on me. He even notified my chairman that I had been offered the position at Mount Sinai, which I had not yet announced. They had a well-attended cocktail party for me at five p.m., with wine and finger food. By seven p.m., the snow had stopped, and it was time to head back over the George Washington Bridge to New Jersey.

That weekend, I was particularly upbeat. I looked forward to my new job at a fine New York City hospital. But this was short-lived. On Monday morning, I received a call from the head of the search committee at Mount Sinai. I was screwed. The president had just initiated a medical center hiring freeze. It was nothing personal, simply a fiscal decision. They decided instead to make the general dentistry director the acting chairman of the department, setting the program back five years.

I had the rug pulled out from under me before I started. I went berserk. They had misled me, using my name and reputation to recruit new applicants. They told my chairman I had accepted the position before I even told him. Fortunately, my chairman had not yet started a search for my successor. With my tail between my legs, I assured him I wasn't going anywhere. Well, I guess after Detroit, I deserved it.

I laid low until 2006, when an ad in the AAOMS classifieds for the chair at Case Western Reserve University in Cleveland, Ohio, caught my eye. Their well-respected chairman was evidently stepping down to become dean of Case Western School of Dental Medicine. He seemed genuinely receptive when I submitted my curriculum vitae to the search committee. Three trips out to Cleveland and countless interviews later, including with the chief of plastics and reconstructive surgery at the Cleveland Clinic, they offered me the position. They flew my wife and me out for a final recruiting visit. The chairman took us to dinner at a beautiful mansion outside of Cleveland and set my wife up with a real estate agent the next day. She checked out the upscale suburbs of Shaker Heights, Pepper Pike, and Solon, where real estate was more reasonable than in New Jersey. I told him that the offer flattered me and I would decide over the weekend. We flew home the next morning in time for me to coach my twelve-year-old son's Little League championship game, where he was scheduled to pitch.

It was a tough decision. My wife was supportive of the move. My mother was now eighty. She had a recent trip and fall, with a resultant broken hip and elbow. My daughters were now well established in high school, with college applications on the horizon. Although Case Western Reserve University had a fine reputation and offered a generous faculty tuition exemption, both girls had their sights set on Ivy League colleges (Columbia and Dartmouth). I notified my chairman of my offer. He wanted to know what he could do to keep me. I said it wasn't a negotiating ploy. Again, he went to the CEO and they came up with a counteroffer. They would give me a large raise exceeding what Case Western was offering. In fact, it had to be approved downtown by Mayor Bloomberg's office. I would be named vice chairman and promoted within the medical school to the rank of full professor. Most importantly, it was agreed that I was in line to become the chairman once the current one stepped down.

Once again, it was not my finest hour. It really hurt me to call the Case Western chair and turn down the offer because we had established a genuine connection. He was gracious and wished me well. Their subsequent chairman selection turned out to be a great guy as is their program director. Oh well, at least I didn't sign a contract this time or buy a house. But academic OMS is a small world. Now, I was done as a serious candidate for a chair position ever again.

As I said before, it is always easier to stay than uproot the family and move. Despite family ties and financial gains, I consider Henry Ford and Case Western the two biggest mistakes of my career. As I've cautioned my residents who seek a career in academics, you must be willing to hopscotch around the country until you find the ideal job if you want to become chairman at a reputable institution.

FRACTURE

After eventually backing out of the Henry Ford Hospital deal, Helaine and I proceeded with renovating our New Jersey home. We planned to install hardwood floors, redo the kitchen, finish the basement, and, most importantly, install an in-ground pool. Due to the slope of our backyard, this would require building a retaining wall into the hill plus landscaping and fencing. All told, the project would cost $60,000. We started in early spring 2002 and completed the pool by June.

Every year since becoming program director in 1992, I hosted a midsummer resident party. Starting in Teaneck and then transitioning to Marlboro in 1996, the party highlights included a softball game at a local town park followed by a barbeque at our house. Residents, spouses, and their kids were invited.

On August 5, 2002, I eagerly awaited our first pool party. With the pool as the center of activity, I decided against the softball game. Instead, the residents started playing three-on-three basketball in the driveway. Unwise at the age of forty-nine, I joined them. Having been a pretty fair ballplayer in my day, I welcomed the opportunity to show off my outside shot. I was holding my own until I went up for a rebound and was crossbody blocked by my six-foot-three 275-pound Israeli kickboxer junior resident. He had never played basketball before. To make matters even worse, he came down with his entire weight on my left leg. In midair, I sensed I was in big trouble. Once I landed, I was shocked to see my foot dislocated at a ninety-degree angle lateral to my lower leg.

I didn't cry out in pain. The endorphins must have kicked in immediately. A couple of residents whisked my then-eight-year-old son inside so he wouldn't see me in my present state. There was no time for an ambulance. A chief resident, with the assistance of a junior resident, picked me up and threw me in the back of his SUV with my ankle in a bucket of ice.

In fifteen minutes after a high-speed ride, we pulled in to CentraState Hospital in neighboring Freehold. On arrival, they transported me on a stretcher into the acute trauma bay. The head nurse assessed my injury. Totally aghast, she turned away and drew the curtain. The emergency medicine physician checked my distal pulses, which were still intact. He offered me Dilaudid for the pain and Zofran for the expected accompanying nausea. As they took me to radiology, they asked if I knew an orthopedic surgeon on staff. I replied that I only knew my plastics colleague who had trained at Kings County. The nurse got him on the phone. He assured me that the orthopod on-call was excellent. In fact, he told me that I would like him because he was as cynical and sarcastic as me.

The orthopedic surgeon arrived within twenty minutes and assessed my injury. I had sustained a trimalleolar fracture dislocation of the left ankle. I had consumed a beer and munched on chips at two p.m. before my accident an hour later. It was now four p.m., so definitive surgery would have to wait until tomorrow for safe anesthesia administration. He offered to give me propofol and reduce the dislocation right then and there in the ER before going to the operating room for definitive surgery the following day. I requested an anesthesiology consult to see if we could avoid a two-step procedure. A female anesthesiologist arrived in minutes. We agreed to do the surgery at six p.m. under spinal anesthesia with IV sedation. If I required general anesthesia to reduce the dislocation, she would proceed to a crash intubation with its inherent aspiration risk. I gladly signed the anesthesia consent.

During the surgical consent, the orthopod informed me of the surgical risks, including fat embolism, deep vein thrombosis/pulmonary embolism, infection, malunion, nonunion, need for secondary surgery, etc. He added, "You could die, but you really have no choice." Yup, he was just as cynical as me.

Everyone in the ER was as accommodating as possible. They even called me Dr. Lazow, which seemed odd as I was now the patient. Then, I looked at the top of the consent form. The patient identification label had it clear as day: Stewart Lazow, DDS. Nope, not Stewart Lazow, MD. Not even Stewart Lazow, DDS, MD. Where had they gotten that information from? I looked at my chief resident in disbelief. I shrugged and shook my head. "Great," I muttered. "If I drop dead on the table, I'll succumb as a freaking dentist."

At six p.m., I kissed my wife and kids as they wheeled me up to surgery. I reminded my wife where all my insurance policies were kept. Next thing I remember, I was in the OR. Versed and fentanyl eased my anxiety as the anesthesiologist administered the spinal, which numbed me up from the waist down. After the propofol infusion was started, I was totally out.

I didn't need intubation. I briefly awakened intraop as the surgeon showed me my now-reduced dislocated ankle. Once I fell asleep again, he placed a plate and five screws in my left fibula, inserted a nail in my left tibia, and sutured my torn ligaments.

I awoke in the recovery room at eight p.m., only five hours after my accident. I was the only patient in RR; after all, it was a Sunday night in a community hospital. I monitored my own vital signs, and every ten minutes the nurse stopped in to ask if I needed more pain meds. The nurse brought my family in to see me in RR. By nine p.m., I told them to go home; I'd see them in the morning. By ten p.m., I was transferred to a nice private room in the new wing of the hospital. The nurses checked my distal pulses every hour and offered me two Percocets every four hours. By midnight, I was dozing off when I heard this shrill scream coming from the room next door: "Sylvia, Sylvia, get me out of here!" It was nonstop all night long.

At six a.m., I announced to the nurses that I couldn't take it anymore. I needed to be discharged home. They informed me that I had to wait for the attending to see me post-op. The orthopod's partner introduced himself at eight a.m. He checked my distal pulses and capillary refill, assuring me that the post-op X-ray taken in the OR showed an anatomic reduction. However, he added that in fifteen years I would probably suffer from arthritis of the ankle. *Great, I'll worry about it then*, I thought. *Nice bedside manner, doc.* He completed the discharge pending a physical therapist teaching me crutch ambulation.

My entire family came to take me home. Transferred from my bed to the wheelchair, the nurse wheeled me past the room of my elderly neighbor who had kept me up all night. Poor guy, he was obviously suffering from dementia and was awaiting surgery for a hip fracture. In the elevator, I told my kids that once I hit the ripe old age of eighty and I sustained my first sentinel event—an unexpected occurrence leading to serious physical or psychological injury—just take a gun and shoot me. My son callously replied, "Do I have to wait till you turn eighty?" Everyone had a good chuckle at my expense, including the nurse. I left the hospital at nine a.m., just eighteen hours after my injury.

My post-op course was essentially unremarkable. Since it was my left ankle that had been injured, I could drive. I was out of work for three weeks, which I spent watching the Little League World Series from Williamsport, Pennsylvania, every day. I returned to work on crutches by week four to perform administrative duties. The residents were less than pleased to have to push me around the hospital in a wheelchair on rounds. I received a lot of attention and empathy from the staff and patients who sensed a kindred spirit.

After three weeks, I asked my surgeon why I was still in a boot. Hadn't he placed a plate and five screws as rigid fixation? After all, when we use rigid fixation in the maxillofacial region, we often allow immediate function. He sarcastically replied, "Yeah, but you don't walk on your face." By week four, he said I could discard the boot if I proved to him I could hop on my leg. No problem. I hopped on my right leg. "Nice try," he laughed. No freaking way I was hopping on my left leg. By week six, I fearfully hopped on my surgically repaired left ankle without pain. It was finally time to discard the boot.

Five months post-injury, my family took a trip to Atlantis on Paradise Island in the Bahamas. Before I fractured my ankle, we were scheduled to travel out West to the Grand Canyon and Sedona. Well, I couldn't go hiking that summer, so we delayed and changed our vacation plans. In January 2003, in response to my kids' persistent dares and with a surgically fixated left ankle, I took the infamous Leap of Faith with its sixty-foot perpendicular water plunge. The next day,

I shot an eighty-four on the Ocean Club golf course. I sent my orthopedic surgeon a copy of the scorecard with my thanks.

SMALL WORLD

Back in 1993, the chairman of plastic and reconstructive surgery at
Kings County-Downstate offered me a residency slot in his program,
pending my completion of an additional year of general surgery. I
turned down the offer for family reasons, but he proceeded to give
me sound advice anyway. He succinctly told me to never trust your
residents without verification. Well, I never took him literally, but one
episode in the early 2000s opened my eyes to his wisdom. This event
sent a lesson to my residents that oral and maxillofacial surgery is a
small world indeed.

Back in 1999, we had an open four-year OMS certificate position
after the match. We took a gamble on an NYU graduate who had
fallen through the cracks of a match process that only rewards 45
percent of the applicants. My colleague at NYU-Bellevue, for whom I
had the utmost regard, raved about him. This NYU graduate became
a gregarious and competent intern.

Everything seemed fine throughout his second year—that is until
I received a phone call from my counterpart at Montefiore Medical
Center in the Bronx. This program director ran probably the best
four-year OMS certificate program in the city; they did not offer a
six-year MD/OMS track. He notified me that he had an unexpected
third-year residency opening. He had already interviewed my resident
for the slot. As a no-nonsense straight shooter, this director assured
me that he wouldn't poach my resident if it would cause a hardship
for our program. Stunned, I told him that this was all news to me. We
had invested a lot in this resident and assumed he would matriculate
at the County for all four years. As a man of his word, the PD with-
drew his offer. I gained a lot of respect for him.

I decided not to tell the resident about the phone call. He

completed his residency at the County in 2003 and became one of our most competent office oral surgeons. At our annual graduation dinner in June, I spoke highly of him. I mentioned in passing that the Montefiore program director, now their chairman, had called to offer heartfelt congratulations to the CR for completing his residency at Kings County. The CR looked like he had just seen a ghost. You see, oral and maxillofacial surgery is a tight-knit community; nothing remains a secret for long.

Fifteen years later, this proud Kings County alumnus is one of our most successful oral surgeons, with four state-of-the-art offices in northern New Jersey. He has taken on multiple partners and associates, including another one of our more recent graduates. He has taken advantage of a practice consultant to position his business in the forefront of the specialty. I even get a chuckle every time I see his face plastered on a huge billboard by the Lincoln Tunnel entrance.

RUSTY

By the summer of 2003, another future head and neck oncology/microvascular surgery fellow would return to the County. After two years off-service in medical school and another year off-service in general surgery residency, this resident was rusty in performing routine office oral surgery. This is why I typically recommend that our six-year MD/OMS residents moonlight while in medical school. Moonlighting during residency outside of work-hour restrictions, whether OMS or general surgery, remains strictly prohibited. In fact, the Committee of Interns and Residents contract states that clearly in black and white. However, there is nothing to prohibit moonlighting while in medical school, as long as it doesn't cause a time conflict. Moonlighting serves the dual purposes of maintaining manual dexterity while working in the oral cavity and providing some semblance of income to offset medical school tuition.

That summer, one of our returning MD/OMS residents had

actively moonlighted while another elected not to moonlight. Unfortunately for the latter resident, he would start the resident year with our newly established six-month rotation to Staten Island University Hospital (SIUH). Under the auspices of Dr. David Hoffman, a Parkland-trained OMS, this rotation would emphasize cleft lip and palate, orthognathic, and TMJ surgery. That was the good news. The bad news was that residents had to provide dental clinic coverage at both SIUH and Maimonides Medical Center. Every Tuesday afternoon, the SIUH rotator would supervise the newbie general practice residents at Maimonides under my auspices while I saw my private patients. This was sheer torture for the resident and me. Most GPRs had little prior experience nor interest in oral surgery. It was a busy clinic that would often back up past the five p.m. witching hour when the excellent support staff would walk out the door, leaving us without dental assistants or instruments.

One Tuesday afternoon in early summer, this particular MD/OMS resident had just returned from his three-year sojourn in medical school and Gen Sx. He had to oversee five GPRs at one time. These GPRs were fresh out of dental school and could be best split into three groups: useless, clueless, and dangerous. My resident was tasked by a nubile GPR to assist in what appeared to be a routine surgical extraction of a grossly carious mandibular premolar. "No problem. I got it," he assured me as I retreated to see a couple of patients in the private suite. One hour later, one of the trustworthy dental assistants summoned me to the clinic. Judging by the number of charts in the to-be-seen bin, the clinic was irrevocably backed up. I then saw my resident appearing totally flustered. His patient, a frail old White lady, had no doubt had a syncopal episode.

Having fainted, she had been placed in the Trendelenburg position with her feet elevated and her head down to increase cerebral blood flow. He administered low-dose oxygen to her via nasal cannula. A wet paper towel had been placed on her diaphoretic forehead. My somewhat embarrassed resident assured me that the patient's vital signs were now stable. Now fully awake and responsive, this lovely lady wanted to complete the procedure. We slowly uprighted the dental chair without recurrent orthostatic hypotension.

I asked the patient to open her mouth. I then removed the gauze that had been placed over the surgical site for hemostasis. I did a double take; I could barely believe my eyes. It looked as if a grenade had exploded in her jaw. Working as expeditiously as possible, I retrieved the retained root and sutured whatever gingiva (gum tissue) was left. The resident prescribed an antibiotic and analgesic. An ice pack to the jaw seemed an appropriate parting favor for having survived the procedure.

As for the embarrassed resident, he was quite trainable over the next two years. Amazingly, after graduation, he went on to complete a head and neck oncology/microvascular surgery fellowship in Maryland. Go figure.

MATRIMONY

Over the past forty years, I have been invited to countless resident weddings. Some residents probably felt compelled, in order to be politically correct, to invite me and my chairman. Others actually hoped I would attend. My wife and I have opted to go to a dozen or so weddings, especially if local in the Tri-State area. If we couldn't make it, we would graciously send a gift. More residents are now getting married during their residency than in my resident years. Moreover, many residents are starting families during their residency, though that does not include our female residents. The reasons for higher rates of marriage during residency are undoubtedly twofold. The residency program has lengthened from three to six years. Most dual-degree residents are in their early thirties by the time they complete the program. Secondly, the threat of HIV, Hepatitis C, and other sexually transmitted diseases has put a damper on the single lifestyle.

On five occasions, one of our OMS residents would marry a GPR from one of our six affiliate hospitals. One such liaison became obvious to the entire department at our monthly meeting at Maimonides Medical Center when a tall Russian OMS resident literally hurdled two rows of seats to sit next to his embarrassed GPR girlfriend.

In 2006, one such wedding never took place. An affable four-year OMS resident, during the spring of his chief year, had mailed out "Save the Date" cards for his anticipated summer wedding upon completion of the program. My wife and I planned to attend. A couple of weeks later, I arrived early at the County for a seven a.m. Tuesday lecture to find him sleeping in the resident room. It seemed odd to me since he hadn't been on-call that night. When questioned, he admitted that he had moved into his fiancée's apartment months earlier. One night after their "Save the Date" mailing, he came home to find she had changed the locks and effectively kicked him out. End of engagement. Oh well. I didn't have to save the date after all nor send a gift.

It should be mentioned that the rigors of a surgical residency place undue stress on a marriage. Eleven of my sixty-one residents got divorced during or soon after residency. A startling three of the eight female residents who completed or were still in the program at the time of my retirement also divorced.

OUTLIERS

By 2007, we had expanded our affiliate hospital roster to include Downstate, Maimonides, Coney Island, Brookdale, Kingsbrook, Wyckoff, and Staten Island University Hospital. The senior residents, third-year residents in our four-year OMS certificate program, and fifth-year residents in the six-year MD/OMS program covered these outliers. None of these affiliates had an OMS residency program. On any given night, these residents could be driving all over Brooklyn covering maxillofacial trauma at multiple hospitals. They had to provide backup for the often clueless GPRs on the frontlines at each institution. On a positive note, they got to run their own service at these outliers and operate with the private attendings on-call there.

Each affiliate hospital had its own quirks. Coney Island, another New York City Health and Hospitals Corporation hospital in Brooklyn, had semiprivatized its surgery department. Interestingly enough, all the general surgery and urology attendings happened to be of Indian descent. In 2007, our senior resident just happened to also be of Indian descent. One day, an OMS attending colleague, my resident, and I had just finished a long case and were walking from the OR to the surgery office to pick up our biweekly paychecks. We ran into the chairman and vice chair of surgery as well as the urology chief. They enthusiastically greeted our senior resident and gladly shook his hand. It was as if my White colleague and I didn't exist. I guess it was a deliberate ethnic diss.

By 2008, our rotation to SIUH was even better established. Our senior residents welcomed the opportunity to scrub in with Dr. David Hoffman on his cleft lip and palate, TMJ, and orthognathic cases. However, the first senior resident assigned during the summer months had the ignominious task of providing backup call for the newly dental school-graduated GPRs. Now, Staten Island University Hospital, like Kings County, had a general dentist as chairman of the dental department. Although our OMS rotation was under the auspices of Dr. Hoffman, director of OMS, the SIUH dental chairman was most concerned with the clinic and on-call coverage of his GPRs. He emphasized to his clueless GPRs that they should feel free to liberally call for OMS backup whenever paged to the ER. This meant that the OMS rotator could travel back and forth over the Verrazano Bridge multiple times per night, paying a ridiculous $12 toll each time. Now, that toll is up to $19.

In summer 2008, our OMS rotator to SIUH felt abused by the GPRs and took matters into his own hands. Rather than write a paper suitable for publication in an OMS peer-reviewed journal, as was our requirement for a certificate upon completion of the program, he produced something quite different. It was a treatise titled, "When Not to Call the OMS Resident for Backup."

Simply put, his rules were:

1. Do not call for minor lip lacerations, minor dental abscesses, avulsed teeth, or anything a GPR or second-year chief GPR should be able to handle.

2. Only call for major facial lacerations, major orofacial infections with impending airway compromise, or facial fractures requiring admission.

Somehow, the SIUH chairman got a hold of a copy of this manifesto from a disgruntled GPR. He went ballistic and immediately contacted my chairman. My chairman went equally ballistic and called me on the carpet to punish my OMS resident. Upon reading the treatise, I could only laugh.

I called my resident and congratulated him on his first and, as it turned out, only publication.

GPRS

Starting in 2007, all applicants for initial dental licensure in New York were required to complete at least one year post-dental school of an accredited clinically based dental residency. This requirement was a windfall for one-year general practice dental residency programs all over the state. Over the next few years, the number of GPR residency positions at Kings County ballooned to ten per year.

As previously mentioned, as far as the OMS residents were concerned, most GPRs fell into the useless, clueless, or dangerous categories. County GPRs were mostly interested in advancing their knowledge and technical skills in those fields of dentistry that they intended to include in their private practice upon completion of the program. These included operative dentistry (fillings), prosthetics (dentures and crown and bridge), endodontics (root canals), periodontics (scaling and gum surgery), pedodontics (children's dentistry), and basic oral surgery (extractions). County GPRs even placed implants under the supervision of the chairman and restored them under supervision of the GPR director.

Most GPRs had little or no interest in more advanced oral and maxillofacial surgery unless they were auditioning for an OMS residency slot. These GPRs dreaded taking calls, especially on nontrauma nights when they were in-house by themselves. This led to some memorable moments. Four come to mind.

One evening, the entire OMS team and the GPR on-call that nontrauma Monday night rounded on a post-op frontal sinus fracture patient. The surgical procedure had entailed a bicoronal flap for access to the forehead. Since it was now post-op day three and his drainage was minimal, we removed the JP drain. We sutured the small drain exit site and placed a pressure dressing over the entire scalp to prevent hematoma formation. Given the vascular nature of the scalp, we emphasized to the GPR in no uncertain terms that he needed to round on the patient at least twice that evening. If the nurses called him overnight and notified him that the dressing had come off, he had to drag his sorry ass out of bed, come see the patient stat, and replace the dressing immediately.

The next morning, the entire OMS team plus the GPR, who was now post-call, rounded on the patient. When we reached his six-bed room, I pulled back his curtain, which elicited a group gasp. The patient's head looked like a lightbulb; the pressure dressing was on the floor. The GPR could only shrug in response to further inquiry. Attempts to evacuate the massive hematoma and control the bleeder under local anesthesia in the clinic were futile. We had no choice but to take the patient back to the OR, where under general anesthesia we raised half the length of the bicoronal flap to gain control of a small branch off the superficial temporal artery.

~

GPRs were not great ambassadors when called upon to communicate with patients' families. One Monday night, again a nontrauma night, the recovery room nurse paged the GPR, on-call by himself, to speak to the immediate family of a post-op patient. The young man had undergone a hemi-mandibulectomy (extensive jaw resection) for an ameloblastoma (a benign but aggressive jaw tumor). We had performed an immediate reconstruction with an allogeneic cadaver mandible (freeze-dried, gamma-irradiated human mandible from a reputable bone bank). We hollowed it out to use it as a crib and packed it with autogenous (the patient's own) posterior iliac crest cancellous bone. Sidebar—currently, one might opt to reconstruct the mandible with an autogenous microvascular free fibular graft (MVFF).

Our team had spent considerable time with the family discussing the treatment plan and obtained all necessary consents for the use of the cadaver mandible. Nevertheless, with the immediate family present at bedside, the mother again inquired as to "What kind of bone did you place in my son's head?" Exasperated, the GPR replied, "I'm not sure. Some kind of animal bone." The mother passed out.

Two weeks after discharge, the patient was readmitted for IV antibiotics to treat a post-op soft tissue wound infection that fortunately didn't jeopardize the bone graft. The mother advised us that he had become infected because the open window in his room at home allowed "the breeze to bring the devil to attack the animal bone in his head."

~

Sex in the resident room was frowned upon, but I suspect it happened more times than I cared to know. Over the years, most participants have remained anonymous, but one resident gloated about his sexual indiscretion. This particular GPR, of Haitian descent, had been courting a dental assistant trainee for weeks. One night when he was on-call by himself, he asked this lovely young lady to stick around after clinic and join him for dinner.

None of his fellow residents suspected anything out of the ordinary. That is, until the next morning, when they returned to see a tablecloth spread over the coffee-stained table in the middle of the resident room, along with the remains of two ivory candlesticks. It didn't take much effort from his colleagues to pry the details of his romantic interlude. As he exited the room, he simply said in his Creole accent, "Zee best pussy I ever had."

Along similar lines, another GPR inadvertently provided comic relief for the patients anxiously sitting in the crowded waiting room during lunch break. It was noon, and all the residents were gathered in the resident room. This GPR was vividly describing a video he had seen the night before of a woman performing oral sex on a horse. Little did anyone realize that someone had left the intercom button activated on the phone in front of him. Suddenly, the front desk receptionist ran into the resident room and breathlessly explained that the whole conversation was being broadcast overhead throughout the waiting room. After lunch broke at one p.m., every male patient was smiling from ear to ear as they came to the back of the clinic for treatment.

HURTS LIKE A MOTHERF*****

Every three years, more than 22,000 US hospitals undergo a Joint Commission on Accreditation of Healthcare Organizations (JCAHO) site visit. This triennial accreditation is required for continued Medicare and Medicaid reimbursement. In preparation for this visit, huge hospitals such as Kings County Medical Center, start gearing up more than six months in advance. As the dreaded date approaches, the level of hysteria and paranoia escalates exponentially. Simulated walk-throughs in each department by paid former JCAHO site visitors are accompanied by the mandatory "suits" and "clipboard" administrators who are only seen every three years.

Having gone through eight such JCAHO site visits, they never fazed me. Somehow, I was always tasked with leading the clinic walk-throughs. The main focus in the Oral Surgery Clinic was always our ambulatory general anesthesia suite. The only time a site visitor ever "dinged" me was when they asked to see the pediatric paddles for our mandatory defibrillator. Taken off guard by the question, I forgot that those paddles were in fact within and under the adult paddles. But, we thankfully weren't cited for my oversight. In fact, I can't remember any major citations in eight such department site visits, and the hospital always received excellent reviews.

The focus of each triennial JCAHO site visit reflected the emphasis of our healthcare delivery system at that time. Two such visits only nine years apart displayed diametrically opposed views. In the late 2000s, the emphasis was on pain control. At that time, pain was considered the fifth vital sign. Every clinic visit and inpatient admission required documentation in the medical record of the patient's subjective pain level. The visual analog scale ranged from one to ten, with a happy face representing a pain score of one and a crying face representing a pain score of ten. Of course, our residents designed their own pain scale after interviewing numerous County patients. On the County pain scale, a score of one was "no fucking pain," a seven was "hurts like a motherfucker," and a ten was "if you ask me again, I'm going to put a cap in your ass."

In 2009, one of our JCAHO departmental site visitors was a lovely retired nurse from the South. She was surprised by our typically packed waiting room since we treated more than 150 patients per day. She sincerely empathized with those people sitting for hours in apparent pain. She offered an analgesic solution they tried in Mississippi. She suggested, with a straight face, that we hand out fentanyl lollipops to people with toothaches. Fentanyl is fifty to 100 times more potent than morphine. It is typically administered either intravenously in a hospital or surgicenter setting or via a patch on an ambulatory basis. I replied that if we offered fentanyl pops to every patient who claimed to be in pain, we would have half of Brooklyn's four million inhabitants lined up outside our clinic every morning.

By 2018, the goal of healthcare had shifted dramatically from focusing on pain control to strict narcotic avoidance to minimize the scourge of opioid overdoses in this country. Our 2018 site visitor, a retired physician, was happy to hear that the Kings County Oral Surgery Clinic was the site of the original Motrin (ibuprofen) pain study performed on wisdom tooth extraction patients in 1979. In fact, I participated in that study my intern year. With the added restrictions on narcotic prescriptions, in 2018 our residents routinely recommended that patients take over-the-counter ibuprofen for mild pain or wrote higher dose Motrin 800 milligrams for every eight hours for moderate pain. Narcotics were withheld unless severe pain was anticipated. Since my name happened to be on every electronic prescription generated in the department, I required residents to use the New York Health Commerce System's I-Stop PMP (Physician Monitoring Program) to check the patient's narcotic history before hitting "send." The site visitor was ecstatic. No fentanyl pops for him.

One such I-Stop PMP computer check on a private patient of mine at Maimonides Medical Center opened my eyes to narcotic shoppers. I had performed an extensive office oral surgery under local anesthesia. I offered the patient prescriptions for an antibiotic as well as Motrin 800. His wife mentioned that Motrin did nothing for him. He couldn't remember the pain medication that worked for him in the past. His wife chimed in that he needed ten-milligram Percocet tablets, not the usual five-milligram dosage, or he would be up all night. Although it was time consuming and an annoyance, I went to the I-Stop PMP website. I couldn't believe my eyes. He had just filled a prescription for 125 x Percocet ten-milligram tablets only two days earlier. When confronted, he now remembered that his worker's compensation physician had prescribed it for lower back pain from a job injury. Much to his chagrin, I e-prescribed Motrin.

I admit that some current wisdom tooth studies claim that high-dose ibuprofen is as effective as narcotics for post-op analgesia. However, from personal experience after my fractured ankle surgery, I can attest that Vicodin and especially Percocet are much more effective for post-op pain. So, I have reached a compromise between the two extremes. Yes, as physicians and dentists, we must be careful to avoid making our patients vulnerable to long-term opioid dependence. But, we also have a duty to adequately treat pain. I continue to prescribe the appropriate narcotic analgesic to relieve severe pain, with a maximum of twelve pills.

OVERDUE

In 1980 during my second year of OMS residency, my chief resident was a female. A mere thirty years later, in 2010, I would graduate my first female resident as program director. She was a seven-year resident who had completed a preliminary OMS internship with us prior to acceptance into our categorical six-year MD/OMS program. She was an outstanding resident— bright and technically strong with sound surgical judgment. She was well liked by her fellow residents, attendings, ancillary staff, and her patients. It came as no surprise to anyone at the County that she was accepted into Dr. Ord's highly competitive fellowship at the University of Maryland. She excelled there and stayed on at Maryland. Presently, she serves as the OMS residency program director as well as associate program director of the head and neck oncology/microvascular fellowship.

Since 2010, we have successfully matriculated eight women residents—a far cry from the previous thirty years. This is consistent with an ever-expanding female applicant pool in our annual OMS match. Perhaps it represents that women currently make up approximately 50 percent of their graduating medical and dental school classes. I have seen this change influence my daughters' career choices as well. My older daughter completed her six years of residency and fellowship training as a pediatric neuro-oncologist. My younger daughter recently completed her seventh year of general surgery residency, with two more years of trauma surgery/critical care/acute care surgery fellowship on the horizon. Overdue, indeed.

Director III: 2011–2018

THE KINGS COUNTY Hospital Oral Surgery Clinic had moved in the late 1980s from "the dungeon" in the B building basement to a new, much larger clinic in the E building Ambulatory Care Center. It occupied half the ground floor, with fourteen operatories, an X-ray room, a clean and a dirty instrument room, and, of course, the GA room. This room was unique in its own right. It was nicknamed the Spasm Dome due to the prevalence of laryngospasms associated with the usage of Brevital, a shorter acting barbiturate than Pentothal (thiopental). The GA room dated back to the 1970s in the dungeon. Historically, it was the purview of the chief residents. After completing four months (currently five months) of anesthesia rotations in the main OR by the end of their junior year, the senior residents would be indoctrinated into the wonderful world of outpatient general anesthesia.

Dentistry has always championed pain control. Dr. Horace Wells, a Hartford dentist, first demonstrated the use of nitrous oxide for tooth extraction in 1844. Soon after, in 1846, Dr. William T.G. Morton's usage of inhaled ether anesthesia for tooth extraction in the Ether Dome at Massachusetts General Hospital was groundbreaking. Oral surgery, of all the dental specialties, has been at the forefront of ambulatory general anesthesia.

For the past ninety years, the single surgeon/anesthetist plus assistant OMS team model has had a remarkably safe track record. General anesthesia mortality rates, cited from oral surgery practices in various states, average one in 400,000 cases. The current OMS team model mandates that the surgeon/anesthetist must have two assistants. One acts as the surgical assistant, and one monitors and observes the patient.

Currently, this team model is under fire by two competing groups with their own financial agendas: dental anesthesiologists and certified nurse anesthetists (CRNAs). Monitoring has come a long way as well. State boards have mandated blood pressure, pulse, respiratory rate, temperature, pulse oximetry, capnography, and EKG with defibrillator monitoring. Our current ambulatory anesthetic intravenous cocktail includes the relatively short-acting medications previously listed: Versed (sedative), fentanyl (narcotic), propofol (general anesthetic), plus the dissociative anesthetic ketamine.

Nevertheless, the GA room serves as the ultimate training ground for the demands of office oral surgery. Our team model in this room calls for a chief resident surgeon, a senior resident anesthetist, a dental assistant, and an OMS attending (director or more often the associate director) supervising the surgery and anesthesia simultaneously. Over my twenty-six years as program director, we averaged more than 600 ambulatory GA cases per year. These were typically performed on Tuesday, Wednesday, and Thursday so as not to conflict with our Monday and Friday OR schedule. Besides learning the art and science of ambulatory deep sedation and general anesthesia, the chief resident was forced to become proficient at wisdom tooth extraction in a timely manner. Fortunately, in my twenty-six-year tenure as program director, having administered more than 16,000 GAs, we suffered no anesthetic fatalities.

Each chief resident brought his or her own level of competence into the GA room. Some were already competent by July 1 of their chief year, while some were absolute torture to observe. But, by the end of their chief year, all were ready for private office oral surgery practice. Over the years, a couple of chief residents were particularly memorable.

One such six-year CR, in 2011, was rather sleuth. In fact, he had flown under my radar for five plus years until one of my Tuesday morning GA room attending sessions. Admittedly, the case involved a difficult, horizontally impacted, mandibular wisdom tooth in a twenty-year-old healthy male referred from Maimonides for surgical extraction under general anesthesia. The crown was buried inferior to the second molar, approximating the inferior alveolar canal on panoramic radiograph. Now, this was years before cone beam CT scans (CBCT) became the standard of care in such cases to help visualize the relation of the tooth to the nerve. The CR obtained appropriate consent from the patient, stating possible procedural complications, including possible paresthesia or numbness of the lip, chin, or tongue.

The CR struggled to section (split) the crown of the tooth from its roots to facilitate its removal in pieces to minimize trauma to the adjacent tooth and neurovascular bundle. I repeatedly asked him if he needed my assistance, which he respectfully declined. After thirty minutes, with sweat pouring off his brow, he reported that he had sectioned the roots and delivered them separately. I looked at the instrument tray on the mayo stand and asked, "Where is the crown?" He said he had drilled it away while sectioning the tooth. Incredulous, I inspected the surgical site but couldn't see anything in the now bloody field. I directed him to pack the site, wake the patient up, and obtain a post-op panoramic radiograph.

He sheepishly returned and pulled the digital image up on the computer monitor. He looked like he had seen a ghost, but X-rays never lie. Virtually impossible even if it had been purposeful, he had surgically extracted both roots and left the entire crown horizontally impacted inferior to the second molar roots.

Still groggy but none too pleased, we notified the patient that we had to go back in to complete the procedure. When I removed the packing, the bleeding had ceased, affording me adequate exposure to see the crown. With the additional space created by the removal of the roots, I teased the crown out atraumatically. I left the resident to close the mucosal incision. Unfortunately for me, the patient followed up every Tuesday afternoon at my Maimonides clinic session for the next two months until he finally healed without any long-term complications.

DIVERSITY

Dating back even before I started my first residency at Kings County in 1979, oral surgery and subsequently oral and maxillofacial surgery were the province predominantly of Jews and Italians. This so-called first "Golden Age" of oral surgery probably reflected two ethnic groups that were tacitly discriminated against by medical school admissions committees. Therefore, Jews and Italians redirected their applications to dental schools that were more receptive to them.

Over the years of my training and time as program director, medical school admissions gradually started to reflect more diversity along gender, racial, and ethnic lines. With this newfound inclusivity in the medical school universe, a secondary shift in dental school admissions and ultimately oral surgery applicants occurred. This, no doubt, also reflected immigration patterns to the United States. It should be noted that regardless of an applicant's country of family origin, we only accepted US citizens and graduates of accredited US or Canadian dental schools into our program. In fact, since 9/11, the medical school component of the dual-degree MD/OMS program only accepts US citizens.

Since early in my tenure as program director in the 1990s, we trained many excellent residents of Iranian descent. Most of them went on to pursue plastic and reconstructive surgery or cosmetic fellowships. Since the early 2000s, we trained three observant Orthodox Jews. Once they received special dispensation from their rabbis to take call on the Sabbath (Friday night or Saturday), they went on to be strong residents. We also trained two fine Black residents and one who surprisingly jumped ship after his medical school component and went into orthopedics.

Since the mid-2000s, we saw a significant increase in Asian and Russian applicants. Ultimately, we matched and trained several such outstanding residents. We trained an almost equal number of Indian, Chinese, and Korean residents. Residents whose families emigrated from the former Soviet Union, or USSR, tended to originate from the republics of Russia, Ukraine, and Uzbekistan. Ironically, those Russian residents who from time to time thought I was too hard on them never knew that my paternal grandfather had emigrated here from St. Petersburg (subsequently Leningrad) at the start of the 1903 pogrom.

Lazovsky was the original version of my last name, which was modified at the time of immigration to this country. Given my own Russian heritage, I tried to overcome any preconceived prejudice. I also knew it was inappropriate to formulate any ethnic generalizations. Nevertheless, I couldn't help but notice two distinct subtypes of Russian residents over the years. Most of those who comprised the first subtype were extremely bright, hardworking, trustworthy, and appropriately aggressive at bringing cases to the OR. The few in the second subtype had what I called a KGB mentality, with the ends justifying the means. Overly aggressive to a fault, a couple were even pathological liars. When confronted in a lie, they would quickly launch into another lie to cover for themselves. This was a trait that made it nearly impossible for me to trust them as chief residents to run our service. Those few residents gave me quite a few gray hairs over the years.

NIGHTMARE

One resident gave me more aggravation than most at the finish line of her residency. While she was likable, bright, and technically trainable, she was every program director's worst nightmare.

I began to suspect this resident of substance abuse. Perhaps I had been blind to the early signs of her addiction. But her behavior became increasingly erratic during her chief year. She would arrive late to the OR and then leave prematurely, allowing the senior resident to close the incision. She would even disappear from the clinic for extended lunch breaks. Her co-chief resident, who evidently had been covering for her for most of the year, finally expressed his concern to me that she had become a threat to herself. I met with the chairman. We agreed that we couldn't allow her to become a danger to our patients, or worse yet, to her future patients if she were to finish the program.

I called her into the chairman's office. We confronted her directly. She denied any form of substance abuse. We had already contacted the hospital's medical director, who advised us on how to proceed. With "reasonable suspicion," it was within the hospital's rights to demand a toxicology screen. Initially, she refused and threatened to contact her Committee of Interns and Residents union representative for due process. When advised that she would be suspended immediately without pay or health insurance if she refused, she agreed to go to Employee Health for the blood toxicology test.

Sure enough, the tox screen came back positive for multiple illicit drugs. It was the middle of May, and she was just six weeks from completing her residency. She already had a great associateship lined up for July. There was a well-established protocol in the resident bylaws for substance abuse. We referred her to the Physician Health Program for New York State. Its Committee for Physician Health (CPH) is a division of the Medical Society of the State of New York. CPH provides nondisciplinary confidential assistance to physicians, residents, and medical students with substance abuse issues.

As long as she entered the program voluntarily, completed the required three consecutive negative tox screens over six weeks, and obtained a psychiatrist clearance, she would be kept on the hospital payroll. She could also maintain her health insurance and complete the residency program thereafter. If she failed to complete the program, CPH would have no choice but to report her to the New York State Medical and Dental Board, which could suspend her licenses. She assured us she would take all necessary steps to seek treatment.

Well, this resident never completed the CPH program. She claimed to have three negative tox screens from private labs, but these were not performed by the authorized state labs. She obtained a clearance letter from her private family physician instead of a state-certified psychiatrist or psychologist. Each time we met thereafter, I told her to get me a letter from CPH stating that she was cleared to return to work and I would find a way to allow her to complete the final six weeks of her residency.

By the time of my retirement years later, this resident who had so much promise had never been cleared by CPH and never completed her OMS residency. Fortunately, she is still alive. She is apparently working in various dental mills as a glorified general dentist, performing extractions and placing implants. What a shame!

The prevalence of substance abuse among healthcare professionals is estimated to be between 1 to 10 percent. Occupational stress and easy access to both licit and illicit drugs can cause devastating consequences. In retrospect, I was fortunate to have run into this situation only once (that I was aware of) in my twenty-six years as program director.

∼

In 2013, two chief residents were memorable for their bedside manner rather than any specific cases. One was Mormon and had four young children by the completion of his residency. To save money, he and his hardworking wife shared one car. Since she drove to work every day, he rollerbladed more than five miles each day from home to the County as well as to our affiliate hospitals. It was scary to see him weaving in and out of traffic on busy Flatbush streets. It was already like driving in a foreign country for automobiles, and the roads were even more dangerous for bicyclists, pedestrians, and rollerbladers. As another cost-saving measure, he literally lived on peanut butter and jelly sandwiches.

Now, this particular six-year MD/OMS chief resident had a wonderful rapport with his patients. With 150 patients to be seen per day in the clinic, however, this was a luxury we couldn't afford. He would review each patient's rather superfluous family history, social history, and travel history in addition to the required medical and surgical history. He would even hold their hands—anything to allay their anxiety and fears. But in the GA room, he would turn into a brute once the patient was unconscious. One case in particular comes to mind, when he attempted to extract a rather stubborn palatally impacted maxillary bicuspid. Using a straight 301 elevator, which is like a small crowbar, he used his entire six-foot-two strong frame to muscle it out. After five minutes of brute force, the tooth popped out and flew clear across the GA room onto the floor. When he put the elevator down on the mayo stand, it was obvious that he had bent the stainless steel elevator in half. A superhuman feat indeed.

Another memorable chief resident that year was the second of three excellent four-year chiefs from the University of Puerto Rico. All had graduated at the very top of their dental school classes and had completed a preliminary OMS intern year. Two had done their audition year at Brookdale Medical Center, one of our affiliate hospitals in those days, while the third had completed a preliminary year at Baylor in Texas. The one from Baylor had been a member of the Puerto Rico women's national volleyball team and played professionally overseas. All three were totally proficient at routine office oral surgery long before their chief years.

This particular CR was a gentle bear. He possessed a remarkable bedside manner, especially with our Hispanic patients. With his conscious patients under local anesthesia, he would spend five minutes addressing them as "Mommy" or "Poppy" in Spanish. Once he had allayed their fears, he would spring into action. He would instantly place them in a headlock and rip the offending tooth out in a matter of seconds. Then, he would say a couple more "Mommies" or "Poppies" to calm them prior to his exit from the treatment room.

∿

The year 2014 brought another unique threesome of chief residents, including the usual two six-year MD/OMS residents and one four-year

OMS certificate resident. The four-year resident was on his own six-year plan. Raised in upstate New York, he had taken time off after college before deciding to pursue a dentistry career. At NYU School of Dentistry, he had been an average student, generously speaking. After dental school graduation, he arrived at Kings County as a general practice resident. During his GPR year, he displayed interest and aptitude in oral surgery. With his mediocre academic record, we suggested that he complete a preliminary OMS intern year. You see, we can train any resident to schlep teeth, but being a successful OMS resident requires a basic and ever-expanding fund of knowledge. This requires a sincere commitment to read and learn. He passed his audition year, and with some hesitation, we offered him a categorical spot in our four-year program.

Over the four years, he displayed remarkable growth. His in-service exam scores improved exponentially until his chief year, when he outscored his two six-year dual-degree colleagues. By graduation, the faculty voted him "Resident of the Year." He also possessed two fascinating traits, including an excellent golf swing, which was of particular interest to me, and a trendy fashion sense.

We have had several excellent golfers pass through the residency program. A handful had even played college golf. First, there were two brothers from Buffalo, separated by several years, who were outstanding golfers in their own right. Then, a young man from Minnesota, although of average height, generated the fastest clubhead speed I had ever seen. He could easily drive the ball 300 yards even before the technology explosion in equipment we are seeing now. I took each of these residents to my golf clubs over the years, where they had the misfortune of having to play with me. In those days, I was an average player at best and made plenty of excuses for my mediocre play. Not until I would retire and move to a gated golf community in Naples, Florida, with two championship courses would I really improve. Under the tutelage of Dr. Jim Suttie, a "PGA National Teacher of the Year" who had worked with former PGA champion

Paul Azinger, I finally improved to a 9.9 handicap index. Truth be told, I have now reverted to a 13.0 handicap.

One day in the late 1990s, I took the younger Buffalo resident and the Minnesota resident out to the Bethpage Black Course on Long Island, which would be the home of two future US Opens and a PGA Championship. Since a professional tournament had been held on the course the week prior to our visit, the rough was four inches deep and the greens ran a twelve on the stimpmeter. Busy in their residency, neither resident had played all spring. No matter, one shot a seventy-four and the other a seventy-eight from the championship tees. I didn't even break 100.

～

One morning in 2014, the fashion-conscious resident had a rude awakening upon his arrival to the resident room. Several copies of a start-up newspaper were spread all over the table in the middle of the room. On the cover appeared a large color photo of said resident in full regalia. Tall and slim, sporting a scruffy beard, he was posed in his black sports jacket that was three sizes too small, no tie, skin-tight jeans, and Ferragamo loafers without socks. That was better than his brightly colored, horizontal striped socks he wore in the winter. The cover story was about this New York City hospital oral surgeon who maintained his trendy fashion sense on a resident salary. He was quoted as describing his style as "Preppy with an edge."

His fellow residents requested autographed copies of the newspaper, which they quickly posted all over the clinic. By lunchtime, he was greeted upon return to the resident room with a life-size image of a skeleton with his cover photo superimposed on its skull—"Preppy with an edge."

～

The 2015 crop of three chief residents uniquely included one six-year MD/OMS resident and two four-year OMS certificate residents. All three were fine in their own right, but one stood out above the others. This Asian four-year resident was also on her own six-year plan. She had traveled cross-country to Kings County in 2009 as a general practice resident from the University of Pacific-Arthur A. Dugoni School of Dentistry in San Francisco. By the end of her GPR year, she expressed an interest in oral surgery, but she wasn't quite sure that she was ready to commit to a four-year OMS residency. We therefore offered her a one-year preliminary OMS intern position. She excelled in this role, so we were pleased to offer her a categorical spot in our four-year program.

During her categorical intern year, she had the misfortune of taking in-house first call for a third consecutive year. Not surprisingly, she became quite adept at handling the typical ER calls, including lacerations, infections, and fractures. But nothing could have prepared her for the memorable stat page to the ER she would receive on a slow trauma night in 2012.

She happened to be on-call with a GPR who would also go on to complete the OMS program in 2017. As was the protocol in those days, an OMS resident was paired on-call with a GPR. The division of labor called for the GPR to handle routine dental emergencies, while the OMS would handle maxillofacial emergencies and inpatient management. After receiving the stat page, they ran together to the ER, located right next door in the new S building. In fact, New York City, under the Giuliani and Bloomberg mayoral administrations, had invested over one half billion dollars into the new Kings County Hospital Center over the previous decade. This included a new 600-plus bed tower in the D building, a renovated Ambulatory Care Center in the E building, and a new ER, OR, and diagnostic center in the S building.

Upon arrival in the ER, they were ushered to the subacute trauma area. There, several physicians and nurses were gathered around a patient behind a closed curtain. The patient was a thin Hispanic male in his mid-twenties with multiple tattoos and body piercings. He was conscious but in obvious discomfort emanating from his groin. Upon ascertaining the history of his present illness, he related that he was an actor of considerable notoriety in gay porno movies. In fact, he had been filming one such movie earlier in the day. As was often the case, the role required him to wear a cock ring at the base of his well-endowed male genitalia. He explained that the primary purpose of said ring was to restrict the blood outflow from the erect penis to produce a stronger erection or to maintain the erection for a longer time. The only problem was that after filming the scene, he could not remove said cock ring from his now engorged penis.

Slowly, the OMS resident and the GPR raised his hospital gown. The female resident gasped. She later recalled to the entire OMS team that his penis looked like a cyanotic newborn baby. Why in the world had OMS been consulted on this obvious urology emergency? The urology resident had suggested an attempt be made to physically remove the ring before he resorted to needle aspiration or phenylephrine injection into the penis. The ER staff had then concluded that only team dental would have the necessary instruments to remove it.

The GPR ran back to the dental clinic and returned with small wire cutters and orthodontic shears to split the ring. After providing enough sedation to facilitate placing one of the beaks of the shears under the gold ring, it was finally time to attempt to section it. The GPR, who was quite buffed, used all his brute force to cut the ring. The OMS resident then carefully pried it off the base of the penis with two needle holders. The patient screamed, first in pain and then in utter relief. Priapism cured.

Fortunately, the female OMS resident wasn't too shell-shocked and went on to finish her residency. She became one of my all-time favorite residents. I suspect this is partly because she reminded me of my daughters, who were busy with their own residencies. Everyone loved her, including patients, staff, fellow residents, and attendings. She was bright, aggressive, and technically strong, with sound surgical judgment as well as a great personality that lit up the room whenever she entered. She went on to become a partner in Dr. Hoffman's SIUH practice, where she continues to work with rotating Kings County OMS senior residents.

As my several controversial "Letters to the Editor" published over the years in the *Journal of Oral and Maxillofacial Surgery* will attest, I am a major proponent of dual-degree training. Still, some of my favorite residents through the years were single-degree OMS residents.

SWAN SONG

During my last years as program director, from 2016 to 2018, I trained and graduated nine chief residents. We were back on track with six dual-degree chief residents and three single-degree chief residents over this time. All nine were fine in their own right, causing me varying degrees of stress. Three of the dual-degree residents went on to head and neck oncology fellowships. One became the first OMS-trained resident accepted into the competitive ENT-head and neck fellowship at Lenox Hill Hospital in New York City. I don't believe this resident ever fully appreciated how many calls had to be made on his behalf to ensure his acceptance into that program. Taken as a whole, these CRs were quite ambitious, with eight passing their oral boards within three years post-graduation.

Two of these CRs left a lasting impression on me. One young Asian male resident from California had played basketball in high school. I always had a slight preference for athletes during the match process. This resident continued playing pick-up basketball during his residency at the Downstate Medical School's gym. One day, he left the clinic post-call at lunchtime. Unexpectedly, he returned to the clinic a couple of hours later with a bleeding gash over his eyebrow. Evidently, a medical student had elbowed him during a particularly rough game. We quickly moved him into a treatment room, and one of his co-residents performed a nice plastic closure of the laceration.

He next displayed his basketball prowess at my 2016 annual summer resident party at my home in Marlboro, New Jersey. In 2012,

Hurricane Sandy had leveled the basketball backboard and pole in my driveway. After fracturing my ankle back in 2002 while playing basketball with the residents, and with my son away at Colgate University, I chose not to replace the backboard and pole. Instead, the residents and I played basketball in my pool, with the basket on the side of the shallow end. Each resident took turns shooting at the basket while jumping off the diving board from forty feet away. One year, I finally made the shot, or at least I thought I did. I had a hunch it was going to be close when I hit the water. When I re-emerged from the eight-foot-deep side, everyone was clapping. Maybe they were pulling the old man's leg. Anyway, my wife confirmed I had sunk the shot. Regardless, this particular resident made not one, but two consecutive forty-foot shots off the diving board. Unlike the rest of us, who heaved the ball as we jumped off the diving board, he managed to maintain perfect jump shot form. Remarkable!

The other memorable CR was the particularly aggressive Russian resident who went on to a fellowship at Lenox Hill. He was bright, technically strong, and well read. No case was radical enough for him. He spent the better part of his chief year lobbying me to undertake a massive reconstruction case.

A lovely young Black female patient in her twenties presented with a striking case of congenital right hemifacial hypertrophy (HFH). HFH is characterized by unilateral enlargement of the hard and soft tissues of the face. She was adamant about her desire for correction and was willing to accept the risks of a major surgery. First, staff took a bone scan to rule out any ongoing bone growth or malignancy. Then, a 3D CT scan was taken to generate a stereolithic model of her face. Virtual surgery was essential to fabricate an alloplastic predominantly titanium CAD/CAM (computer-aided design/computer-aided manufacturing) total right TMJ.

The surgery was extensive. Step one: a LeFort I osteotomy to level her maxilla. Step two: a left sagittal split osteotomy (SSO) to allow rotation of her mandible back to midline. Step three: resection of her grossly enlarged right mandibular condyle and ramus. This required placement of a vessel loop as a precaution around the right external carotid artery due to a massively dilated internal maxillary artery in juxtaposition with her huge mandibular ramus. Once we completed this most risky part of the surgery, we rotated the mandible back to midline and placed it in intermaxillary fixation (IMF—jaws wired shut). The left SSO was also rigidly fixated with three bicortical screws. For step four, the TMJ fossa implant, with its ultra-high-molecular-weight polyethylene articulating surface, was secured to the undersurface of the zygoma with four screws. In step five, the CAD/CAM TMJ/ramus unit was inserted and secured to the horizontal body of the mandible with five custom screws. Step six: We used the prefabricated surgical guide to resect the excess inferior border of the mandible to midline. Step seven: The IMF was released and the pre-planned occlusion was confirmed. The CAD/CAM condyle, with its chrome-cobalt articulating surface, rotated freely within the fossa implant. Step eight concluded with plastic closure of the two lengthy incisions. Tracheostomy was considered but deemed unnecessary, though the patient was transferred to the SICU for airway observation.

The patient's post-op course was unremarkable. She started post-op TMJ physical therapy soon afterward. She was ecstatic with her result. Once most of her edema had resolved by one month post-op, she gladly agreed to film a video, which was shown on the hospital website.

One year later, we brought her back to the OR for the secondary soft tissue reduction I had promised her. First, we had to replace one of the fossa screws that had loosened under function. That turned out to be no simple task, utilizing a much smaller preauricular incision this time around with much less exposure. Once we had replaced the mobile screw with a larger custom screw, we redirected our attention to her soft tissue. We carried out a buccal fat pad reduction intraorally along with reduction of redundant oral mucosa. Pleased with the result, we discharged her later that afternoon from the ambulatory surgery suite. It was the last surgery of my career.

See Ya!

SURGERY IS A young person's game. The residents are always rightfully pushing the envelope and trying to expand the scope of surgery. Once I hit sixty-four years old, I was ready to leave that to them. I started to plan my exit strategy. Several factors contributed to me considering retirement.

Financially, I would be able to comfortably retire at sixty-five. One of the benefits of having turned down those three chairman offers meant that I had stayed at Kings County with its robust retirement plan. Years earlier, I was smart enough to "buy back" my years as a part-time attending, converting them to full years of service. By sixty-five, I had accrued more than twenty-six full-time years of service in the New York City Employees Retirement System (NYCERS) pension system. Essentially, I had almost maxed out with an accrued pension allowance over 50 percent of my final three years' average salary.

I met with a retirement adviser in the human resources department who wisely set me on the proper path. I visited NYCERS at Jay Street in downtown Brooklyn. Quickly, I realized that NYCERS was perhaps the most efficient bureaucratic agency I had dealt with at Kings County or NYCHHC over the past forty years. They pulled up my computerized records on the spot and confirmed my estimates to the penny.

The price of commuting fifty miles each way to work every day had become exorbitant. Between gas, parking at the two hospitals, and tolls on the Verrazano Bridge, Outer Bridge Crossing, and Garden State Parkway, my daily commuting cost was more than $50 per day. The wear and tear on my car and my psyche was incalculable as I drove more than 32,000 miles per year. My daily commute into the bowels of Brooklyn, which took one hour and fifteen minutes each way when I first moved to Monmouth County twenty-three years before was now more than two hours each way. I had lived through five years of construction on the Staten Island Expressway and Gowanus in Brooklyn. The engineers had failed to consider the simple fact that even if you add another lane to the expressway, the merge at the Verrazano Bridge would still cause a bottleneck.

To make financial matters even worse, my incentive to continue performing complex private cases as part of my faculty practice at Downstate and Maimonides had all but evaporated. Our failed healthcare delivery system now placed almost all medical decision-making in the hands of the insurance companies. They also controlled the fee schedules.

For example, if a patient was referred to me to do corrective jaw surgery, I anticipated countless hours on the phone seeking preauthorization from their insurance company. Even if the patient presented with an obvious skeletofacial deformity, the insurance company would initially reject the case on the grounds that it was cosmetic in nature and not medically necessary. Ultimately, after submitting radiographs, cone beam CTs, photos, dental models, and the virtual surgical treatment plan (none of which the insurance covered), they might reconsider. After six months and countless phone calls, they might occasionally preauthorize the surgery—with one caveat, that is . . .

Most insurance companies typically paid less than one third of my standard fee. If I participated with the patient's insurance company, I was forced to accept their paltry fee as payment in full. If I was out of network, the patient could still opt to have me do the surgery. However, they were responsible for my entire fee less the paltry sum their insurance would reimburse them. Most patients couldn't afford it. So, I would end up doing the case at the County as a "service case," or I'd refer the patient elsewhere. A service case in a public teaching hospital meant the patient was admitted to our OMS service. The patient was not my private patient. Nor could I bill the patient on a fee-for-service basis. The hospital would bill the patient's insurance company (if he or she had hospital coverage) for the hospital stay on a diagnosis-related group (DRG) basis. It just wasn't worth the aggravation anymore.

Perhaps the biggest transformation in the healthcare delivery system I've witnessed over my forty years is the change in the medical practice model. We've transitioned from solo physician private practice to group private practice to hospitals buying up multiple physician groups under one large group umbrella. This gives the hospitals control over hospital referrals, diagnostic testing, and admissions. These hospitals have merged into huge consortiums, which gives them the bargaining power to better negotiate with the health insurance companies over admission and DRG payments.

For example, Northwell Health, a nonprofit integrated healthcare network, is New York State's largest healthcare provider and private employer, with more than 74,000 employees. Its network of twenty-three hospitals includes Long Island Jewish Medical Center, North Shore University Hospital, Lenox Hill Hospital, and both Maimonides Medical Center and Staten Island University Hospital, where our OMS residents rotated.

The implications of this new medical practice model are overwhelming. Basically, the health insurance companies and the hospital consortiums control the purse strings. For those physicians who anticipate working in tertiary hospital academic settings, the hospital controls their salaries and sets their ceilings. As I've told my daughters, "The Golden Age of Medicine is long gone." Unless, of course, your practice includes cosmetic surgery or dental implants performed in an office or private surgicenter on a fee-for-service basis (no insurance).

Then, of course, there were the tax implications. I will try to stay apolitical. President Trump, in an obvious attempt to stick it to the blue democratic states on either coast that didn't vote for him in 2016, came up with the SALT regulation. This capped state and local tax deductions at $10,000. New Jersey already had some of the highest state and real estate taxes in the country, and this made it even worse. Moving to a state without state income tax and reasonable property taxes was becoming more and more attractive.

Then, there was the aggravation quotient at work. The regulation and compliance issues were becoming all-consuming. First, there was HIPAA—the Health Insurance Portability and Accountability Act— to protect patients' privacy. Then, there was the JCAHO site visit every three years and the CODA site visit every five years. Against my better judgment, I had stayed for the 2017 CODA site visit, which had required six months of torture to compile the exhaustive self-study residency program analysis. We passed again with no citations or recommendations. Then, there were the weekly online compliance courses on every topic, from risk management to opioid dependence to infection control and so on. Not to mention, I was also the department quality assurance administrator in charge of monthly mortality and morbidity reports.

My favorite was the electronic health record (EHR). In general, I agree with the concept of increased attending responsibility for patient care, but this became absolutely ridiculous. As director of service, I dedicated my first hour every morning to signing off on every admission note, discharge note, consultation, progress note, ER note, medication reconciliation, lab test, X-ray, and CT scan report for our inpatients from the previous day. This was in addition to signing off on every clinic note for eighty oral surgery patients per day.

Fortunately, the additional seventy general dentistry patients per day were not within my purview. Every day, I received multiple phone calls from local pharmacies regarding prescriptions my residents had electronically prescribed with my name on each one. If only I could have just focused on patient care, resident training, and performing surgery, I probably would have stayed.

As my sixty-fifth birthday approached, it became obvious to me that I would only stay on if I was named department chairman. My longtime chairman had just turned eighty—NYCHHC has no mandatory retirement age. That is probably why I was surrounded by so much dead wood at our monthly medical board meetings.

Over the past quarter century as program director, my chairman and I had painstakingly formed a superficially amiable coexistence. After the last CODA meeting in November 2017, I told him we needed to schedule an hour-long meeting without phone calls, pages, or intercom interruptions. I suspect he anticipated what was on my mind.

The mood was somewhat somber but not adversarial. After appropriate greetings and salutations, I got right to it. First, I noted the progress we had achieved for the department over the past twenty-five years. Then I told him it was my longtime goal to be department chairman. I politely explained that for the good of the department, I would be a far better chairman at sixty-five than he was at eighty. I suggested he stay on as chairman emeritus and continue to train his GPRs in implantology. He didn't freak out or raise his voice. He was well aware of my aspirations. He stated that he had earned the right to retire on his own terms, after the opening of the new clinic. This new clinic had been in the pipeline for years. Architectural plans had been okayed by the administration. The only stumbling block was the $24 million price tag. (As of this writing, no construction has been started.)

By this point, he became increasingly irate. As if to provide a timeline, he told me his plans. "I have no intention to retire in the next two years. Not even in the next five years. If it makes you feel better, I don't see myself working beyond the age of ninety."

I pressed on. I told him that the chairman position was not a lifelong appointment. I cynically offered some historical context. "You are not a Supreme Court justice." In fact, only the oldest judge, Oliver Wendell Holmes Jr., stayed on the bench until age ninety. "You are not the Pope." In fact, the oldest pope, Pope Leo XIII, was ninety-three when he died during his papacy.

What chutzpah he had? What unmitigated gall? There was no turning back now as I walked out the door. I summoned the words of longtime Yankee announcer Michael Kay: "See ya!"

ADIOS

IN MID-MARCH 2018, one of my friends gave me a countdown calendar. I set it to 100 days, which would end on June 30, my official retirement day. I placed it, in plain view, on my desk at the County.

I had a lot to do over my final 100 days. My retirement coordinator in human resources showed me the complex roadmap to retirement. I would first need to file an application with NYCERS. Then I was required to submit a formal retirement receipt to my employer. It was imperative that I could be confident in my pension and continued benefits, especially health insurance for my wife and me. Fortunately, my kids were now "OTP" (off the payroll) and had their own health insurance through their own jobs. Margot was at Cincinnati Children's Hospital, Stefanie was at Beth Israel Deaconess Medical Center in Boston, and Zachary was at the Federal Reserve Bank in New York City.

I also had to retire from Maimonides Medical Center, which created more paperwork. I sent a form letter to my private patients at Maimo, advising them of my impending retirement and arranging their referrals to appropriate colleagues. I also had to box my private patient charts dating back seven years, as per medicolegal guidelines.

Then, there were the retirement parties. Every year for the past thirty-nine years we have held our Annual Alumni Scientific Session and Residents' Day in late June at the chairman's country club in Mamaroneck, New York. This year it was scheduled for June 21, and I was to be the honoree. I decided to throw myself a retirement dinner the very next night on Friday, June 22. I emailed all sixty-one former residents that I had trained to completion and invited them to make a weekend of it—come to the outing on Thursday and stay for my retirement dinner Friday night.

The Thursday outing was fun as usual. A lecture by one of our recent OMS graduates who had just completed his head and neck/microvascular reconstruction fellowship was eye-opening in its scope. Lunch was then followed by a round of golf and a quick shower. Then, we had cocktails and cigars overlooking the beautiful Long Island Sound. We followed dinner with my usual hail and farewell speech about the graduating chief residents. This time, I had to add my own farewell speech and perhaps I got a bit too emotional. As I drove home, I promised myself to keep the festivities on a lighter note at my retirement dinner the next night.

Friday was my last OR day at the County. The residents kept my schedule light knowing that I had my dinner planned for that evening. I got out of the OR early after completing the minor secondary revision on my hemifacial hypertrophy patient, changed, and headed into downtown Manhattan. I arrived at my favorite steakhouse, Wolfgang's in Tribeca, by six p.m. I had reserved the large private banquet room. My son, Zach, walked over from his apartment in Battery Park. The sommelier took him to the wine cellar, where he picked out a nice $2,000 magnum of red wine. Helaine and our older daughter, Margot, who had flown in from Cincinnati, arrived minutes later. My younger daughter, Stefanie, couldn't make it, as she was stuck on-call in the SICU at Beth Israel Deaconess.

Soon, my guests started to arrive. Besides my immediate family, I had limited the invitations to my former residents. I was deeply touched by the forty alumni who attended from all over the country. Some flew in from as far as California, Nevada, Illinois, Minnesota, Texas, and Puerto Rico.

I managed to keep my speech more upbeat this time. I opened by noting that I hadn't received so many gifts since my bar mitzvah fifty-two years before. I then asked all the alumni to introduce themselves as they spanned over twenty-six years of the program. No, I didn't seek their testimonials but rather a synopsis of the year they graduated from the County, any additional fellowships or degrees they had completed, and the type of practice they had pursued. I told them why I was retiring and my plans. I assured them that I would be living vicariously through their accomplishments and those of my children. By midnight, it was time to gather my gifts and pack up the car. It was a tearful farewell as I left to a surprise, though heartfelt, standing ovation. It had cost me a fortune to throw my own retirement party, but it was worth it.

Over the next final week, I packed up my offices at Kings County and Maimonides. I emptied my desks and took down my plaques and diplomas. Thursday was a doubleheader. I catered a lunch at noon for the Maimo staff and then ran back to the County for a department retirement party. Everyone was there including our administrator and even the hospital CEO. They all gasped when I told them I wasn't going to miss the County since the aggravation quotient had become too overwhelming. But they all applauded when I assured them I would miss all the people who made Kings County the "County." This included my colleagues, attendings, residents, dental assistants, nurses, support staff, and, most of all, the patients who I had tried my very best to treat well for the past forty years.

My last day at work, Friday, June 29, arrived. I brought in dozens of bagels and cream cheese for the OR nurses. I thanked them for all their help and support over our many years together. I transitioned the program director responsibility to my former resident, now my successor, who was chomping at the bit to take over my office. However, he was nice enough to give me a very generous parting gift in the form of a gift certificate for a new set of golf clubs. I wished him well and assured him that he would grow into the position over time, as I had done twenty-six years earlier.

As I left my office for the last time, I reflected back to the day when my first chief resident, the "Mayor," graduated in 1980. It was a lesson that would stay with me for the next thirty-eight years.

One of my two chief residents from my intern year was a physically imposing Black man, a former high school all-American linebacker.

He seemingly knew every nurse, technician, and administrator. He was like the mayor of Kings County. I couldn't imagine how in the world the hospital could function without him after his graduation on June 30. Much to my surprise, July 1 came and it was clearly obvious that he was utterly replaceable. The County didn't miss a beat. Yes, I too was utterly replaceable. The County would go on.

It was anticlimactic as I turned in my ID badge to the security office. I hugged my favorite hospital policeman, who always had my back. Then, there were a couple of handshakes, goodbyes, and even an "adios"—forty years to the day!

Scorecard

MY TIME ON the general surgery service taught me that it always comes down to the numbers, being objective rather than subjective. A retrospective objective analysis of my twenty-six-year tenure as Kings County program director tells the tale.

I had the privilege of training sixty-one residents to completion. This included an almost equal number of single and dual-degree residents. At the time of this writing, forty-five of the sixty-one residents (74 percent) have passed their boards, becoming Diplomates of the American Board of Oral and Maxillofacial Surgery. Several more are still waiting to take their oral certification examination. Twenty-two have gone on and completed fellowship training, including seven in head and neck oncology, four in plastics or cosmetic surgery, and eleven in orthognathic/TMJ surgery. Several former residents have gone into academia, with five serving as residency program or fellowship directors with chairman potential.

As for me, I have published thirty-three articles in peer-reviewed journals and written eight book chapters. I have presented more than 100 invited lectures at international, national, state, and local meetings. My residents presented oral abstracts or poster sessions at twenty-five consecutive AAOMS annual meetings. My mandible fracture protocol, based on more than 3,000 fractures successfully treated at the County with less than a 3 percent complication rate, was published and taught at board review courses. I even had the unwanted distinction of being considered something of an expert on the lethal triad of necrotizing fasciitis, mediastinitis, and brain abscess of dental etiology, having lost a patient to each.

On a personal note, I was offered the chairman position at

three well-respected medical centers. In 1996, I became only the twenty-eighth OMS in the country to be granted Fellowship in the American College of Surgeons. I was an American Board of OMS examiner. I remain a manuscript reviewer for three respected journals. Yes, I could have done more if I'd had a true mentor. Still, it was a good run; in sum, forty years at the County.

Epilogue

BACK IN THE winter of 2016, before I had even contemplated retirement, Helaine and I vacationed in Florida. Most years, we had stayed on the East Coast, from Sunny Isles to Boca Raton to her parents' house in West Palm Beach. This time we tried southwest Florida. We split our week between Naples and Marco Island. We even hooked up online with a Coldwell Banker real estate agent who arranged to show us around Naples. It was only a preliminary feasibility study for us.

Instantly, I fell in love with Naples. The saying goes "you can't be too old or too rich in Naples." It has the fifth highest per capita income in the United States and is home to six billionaires. Pristine white beaches off the Gulf of Mexico. Fantastic climate year-round. World-class shopping and dining on Fifth Avenue and Third Street. Over 100 challenging golf courses. Fantastic boating and fishing. Most of all, it presented a welcome change for me from the transplanted New Yorkers of the East Coast to the friendlier Midwesterners of the West Coast.

I kept Naples in the back of my mind as a retirement destination. After the decisive meeting with my chairman at the end of 2017, I called our real estate agent and advised him that my wife and I would be visiting Naples the second week of January 2018. It was only four months after Hurricane Irma, a category five hurricane, had made landfall on Marco Island. Naples was spared the anticipated water surge and had relatively recovered by the time of our arrival. This time, we told him that we were serious buyers and knew exactly what we were looking for.

It took a full two days traversing Naples back and forth checking out homes until we decided on Twin Eagles, a gated golf community with 714 homes on 1,115 natural acres with two championship courses. Rather than buying a resale, we decided to build a new home that supposedly would be ready by mid-July. We selected the builder, the lot, and the model and picked our upgrades. There was no looking back now.

That gave us six months to sell our home in New Jersey. No shortage of aggravation ensued. Interview three real estate agents, select a real estate agent, have an interior designer stage the house, paint the interior and exterior of the house, and produce a virtual tour of the house. We put the house on the market in April. The real estate market was slow until I decided to open the pool early in the middle of May. Then we received multiple offers and sold for the fair market price. We agreed on a July 2 closing date. That's when the real torture began over the buyer's engineer findings and the Township of Marlboro Certificate of Occupancy inspection. Somehow our real estate agent helped guide us to the finish line on time.

Concurrently, things were getting more complicated in Florida. Midway through June, conversations with our builder in Twin Eagles made it abundantly clear that our house wouldn't be finished until September. Staying for two months in a motel with our dog was unacceptable. I asked if they had a "spec" house available that we could buy instead. They happened to have one just two lots over from our site, the color a hideous mustard yellow. The builder offered us a painting allowance if the homeowners association okayed it. The HOA granted us permission to paint it the tan with white trim of our original house. The spec house had even more upgrades, which the developer threw in at no extra cost. Done deal.

I guess I still had a surgeon's personality. After retiring on June 29, we packed up the house over the weekend. We needed two 1-800-Got-Junk trucks to discard everything we weren't taking to Florida. After all, we were downsizing. Mayflower Interstate Van Lines moved us out of the house by two p.m. on Monday, July 2, just in time for the buyers to do their final walk-through prior to the three p.m. closing.

The moving company would take the better part of a week to get to Florida. So, we stayed in a motel in nearby Freehold, New Jersey, next to the mall for four days. By Friday morning, we picked up our dog—a sixty-five-pound Goldendoodle named Harley—from the kennel and departed for Florida. Our younger daughter, Stefanie, had graciously agreed to take a couple of days off and accompany us on the 1,300-mile two-day voyage to Naples. Stef split the driving with me, while Helaine sat in the backseat with Harley, who we sedated for the trip.

Friday night, we stayed in a dog-friendly hotel in beautiful Florence, South Carolina. After an early start the next morning, we arrived in Naples by eight Saturday night. We stayed in the Hawthorne Suites by Wyndham, also a nice dog-friendly hotel.

Unbeknownst to us, Collier County had not yet granted the final COO, so we couldn't close on our new home in Twin Eagles. Evidently, there was an issue with the front door, which the builder finally replaced. Then the county inspector, who was overwhelmed by hurricane construction permit requests, was delayed for our final inspection. Not to worry, the Van Lines with all our furniture and most of our clothing, was nowhere to be found. Evidently, the moving van made an unexpected stop before us. Finally, after a lovely week sojourn at the Hawthorne, we coordinated the walk-through, the closing, and the delivery of our furniture.

By July 14, we were finally all moved into our new home. I guess it was a lot to coordinate, even with my type A personality. Retire June 29, pack, sell house, and move out July 2. Drive to Florida. Close on house, and move in July 14. It finally hit me. I was officially retired and a full-time Florida resident!

Addendum

PEOPLE ASK ME all the time if I miss being a surgeon. "Not at all," I'm quick to respond. Another OMS I met playing golf shared his own take on retirement: accepting professional irrelevance. I loved Twin Eagles from day one. Only 40 percent of the community are year-round residents, like we were, the first year. The other 60 percent are "snowbirds" or "seasonal" as we prefer to be called. Almost all of the 40 percent would rush on to their computers two weeks in advance to sign up for early tee times via the golf lottery system to avoid the summer heat and humidity. I had no problem with the ninety-five-degree heat and 99 percent humidity every day. I would often play by myself at two p.m. and finish all eighteen holes in two and a half hours, with an electric golf cart of course. I would even sweat off three pounds per round but regain them with a couple of Blue Moons at the tiki bar afterward. I would rush home and jump into my pool and spa before the daily rainy-season five p.m. thunderstorm would hit.

We met several fellow permanent residents at Tiki Tuesday dinners, complete with free cocktails and a DJ. The average age of the community is sixty-four, but these folks are active and love to dance. Then there was the monthly Saturday Trivia Nights in the 47,000 square foot clubhouse. Our table always finished next to last.

As quickly as I acclimated to Florida, Helaine did not. She couldn't handle the summer heat and humidity. She missed her friends back in New Jersey. Our kids were spread around the country in Cincinnati, Boston, and New York City. They weren't planning to visit until Thanksgiving.

Then there was the minor issue of the "creatures" as Helaine less than affectionately called them. As you enter the community past the gatehouse onto Twin Eagles Drive, a sign reminds visitors that "we share the courses with the wildlife." Our house even backs onto a preserve.

Every night, I would walk the dog before I went to bed around midnight. This late shift was my sole canine responsibility as Harley was clearly Helaine's dog. The later I walked Harley, the later she would let my wife sleep in the morning. One August night, Harley took two steps out the front door, stopped in her tracks, and started barking. I looked to my right and saw a cracked open coconut in the driveway. I looked up to the palm tree just right of the driveway and noticed the other coconut that had been growing on the tree was also missing. Maybe the wind had knocked them off the tree. Then I couldn't believe my eyes when I saw a six-foot, 300-pound fully grown black bear drinking the other coconut about fifteen feet from us.

Fortunately, the bear seemed more intent on finishing the coconut milk than us. I slowly backed Harley into the house so as not to arouse the bear. I immediately called gate house security, which told me there was nothing they could do but that I should call the Florida Fish and Wildlife Conservation Commission (FWC) in the morning. I had a shot of Jameson Irish Whiskey to calm my nerves.

The next day, I contacted the FWC and asked if they could possibly sedate and relocate the bear. The agent on the phone laughed. He proceeded to give me a bear tutorial. He advised me that there are 4,000 Florida black bears and they are a protected species in the state. The FWC would only intervene if I filed a documented bear attack, which is exceedingly rare. It seems that the Florida black bear, unlike the brown or grizzly bear, is generally shy and reclusive. It is mostly an herbivore and needs to consume upward of 20,000 calories per day prior to a soft hibernation in the warm Florida winter. The black bear has a remarkable sense of smell up to a mile away, so don't put your garbage out overnight. They can even climb a light pole and run at speeds up to thirty miles per hour.

I asked the FWC agent if I could purchase a gun, like seemingly everyone else in Florida owned, and shoot the bear if he menaced me.

He told me if I shot the bear in the back, I would be arrested because, again, he is a protected species. Evidently, the bear had more rights than me. The agent suggested I buy a signal horn because black bears will run when they hear a loud noise.

After that, I always carried a signal horn when walking the dog. A couple of weeks later, I had my second bear encounter. Around midnight, I exited the house to check that the coast was clear to walk Harley. I heard a noise from behind a dumpster between the four houses under construction next to mine. In fact, one of the houses was the one I had originally purchased. Fortunately, a street light illuminated the area. The construction workers had a habit of tossing their lunch leftovers into the dumpster. The bear thought it was a smorgasbord. He was standing on his hind legs behind the dumpster. Now, he saw me. First, he ducked down, then he stood up. He was playing hide-and-seek. I was certain it was my bear from the other night by the distinctive brown markings on his snout.

I saw my bear several more times as he would exit an opening in the preserve behind my backyard. My wife even spotted the smaller mama bear, with her cub, running across our backyard. Once the four new houses were completed and the dumpster carted away, I never saw my buddy again.

Then there was the alligator. There are an estimated one million alligators in Florida. They prefer freshwater or brackish habitats, while their more aggressive cousins, the crocodiles, favor saltwater. Twin Eagles has multiple lakes around the golf courses that serve as home to the many alligators.

Helaine arrived in Twin Eagles as a golf beginner. We were playing nine holes on the Eagle course with another couple in a late Friday afternoon "nine and dine." I followed the cart path between the lakes to the ladies' tee on the par-3 eighth hole. Evidently, we didn't see the message pop up on the GPS monitor—"alligator on 8th tee"—nor hear the other couple screaming behind us. My wife exited the right side of the cart and almost stepped on the thirteen-foot alligator's head. Fortunately, he scampered back into the lake without taking a bite. She needed an immediate "wine and dine."

There are also countless white-tailed deer around the community. Slightly smaller and much cuter than their northern brethren, especially the spotted fawns, they walk through our backyard grazing on our impatiens. At least they don't carry Lyme disease like in the Northeast.

Then there are the particularly ornery Florida wild turkeys, who flock together around the golf courses. During mating season in the spring, the males, or toms, will fan out their colorful tails and gobble to attract hens. Unfortunately, the Florida wild turkeys have a nasty habit of pecking at their reflection on the side of my previously black car. Of course, there are the occasional bobcats, panthers, and wild boars as well.

Between the summer climate, "creatures," missing her friends and family up north, plus my quick acclimation to the Florida lifestyle, Helaine and I were at a serious impasse. I finally agreed to move back North for subsequent summers. We agreed to be "seasonal"—eight months in Florida and four months in New Jersey.

We drove back to New Jersey on June 1 with Harley again sedated in the backseat. We rented an apartment in our old town of Marlboro. I contacted our real estate agent who had sold our house a year earlier. We looked at several condo units before putting in a bid on a two-bedroom, two-bath apartment in a nice condo community only five miles from our old house. We closed on the condo in mid-September. Much renovation was necessary. New hardwood floors, a fresh paint job, quartz countertops, a backsplash, and all new kitchen appliances needed to be done before we moved in. There was barely time to get settled in before heading south to Florida in mid-October for the next eight months, as per our agreement.

This time, things were different in Florida for my wife. She made new friends. She played golf with the nine-hole ladies, played mahjong, participated in morning water aerobics, and took classes in the fitness center. She even joined the Jewish Federation of Naples and went on their monthly trips. We saw shows at the Artis Naples and Barbara B. Mann Performing Arts Center in Fort Myers. Happy wife, happy life. My biggest concern all winter was buying a wool ski cap at the Golf Pro Shop before my eight a.m. tee time in rare forty-two-degree temperatures for the Mayor's Cup tournament.

COVID-19

PART I

Life was good, then all hell broke loose in early 2020. In March, the Covid-19 pandemic halted life as we knew it. Shelter in place orders issued by our Trump acolyte, Governor Ron DeSantis, haven't really affected my lifestyle. I still drive five miles each way, toking on my pipe, to Straight from New York Bagels (the new owner is actually from New Jersey). I wait in line wearing my surgical mask and practice social distancing by standing six feet behind the lady in front of me. I utter "nice mask" to any Trump stooge who refuses to wear one as a political statement, in direct opposition to the sign on the door requiring it. Take-out only, so I eat in my car.

I walk nine holes of golf, with the pushcart I ordered online, in the ninety-four degree heat every other day. Electric carts have not yet been allowed back on the course. The cups are raised on the greens, which helps my putting. You can't take the pins out to avoid spreading the virus by manual contact. The days I don't play golf I ride my bicycle around the community with my mask on. Then it is home for a swim and spa. Guess the chlorine kills the virus. I do curbside pick-up for dinner from our favorite restaurants that remain open for take-out only, such as pizza from New York Pizza and Pasta, Chinese food from O'mei, or burgers and onion rings from Brooks Burgers (supposedly the number two rated burgers in the country). Then I sit out on my lanai, having a cocktail and smoking my pipe.

The phone rings. It's one of the kids checking up on us. One benefit of the pandemic is that we hear from our kids more often than once per week since we're technically in the vulnerable age group. Margot still treats her pediatric neuro-oncology patients at Cincinnati Children's

Hospital. Fortunately, the Children's Hospital has very few cases. Stefanie is covering a Covid ICU at Beth Israel Deaconess. She thinks she had the virus in February, when she had a persistent URI. And Zach and his girlfriend left the epicenter of the virus in New York City to stay with her parents in Cincinnati. They both work from home for the Federal Reserve Bank and American Express, respectively.

In April, since I still hold an active New York medical license, Governor Andrew Cuomo emailed me a personal invitation to come out of retirement to assist during the peak of the pandemic. I graciously declined since I am now a Florida resident. However, I replied that if they still needed me when I planned to return in July, I would gladly offer my services. I never heard back.

Then, before bedtime, it's time for the wife and I to watch one of our favorite shows on HBO, Showtime, Prime, or Netflix. I take Harley out at midnight. I look over my right shoulder for my buddy Mr. Bear. At least he doesn't have to live in fear of contracting this deadly virus.

PART II

It's Thanksgiving 2020. I have a lot to be thankful for. To date, our family has been spared the horrors of Covid-19, which has infected more than 14,000,000 and killed more than 300,000 Americans. It didn't have to be that way.

Margot was recruited by her mentor to join her at Nationwide Children's Hospital in Columbus, Ohio, starting in July. Stefanie finished two research years at Boston Children's Hospital and resumed her fifth year of general surgery at Beth Israel Deaconess. Zach and his girlfriend, Betsy, got engaged, although the wedding probably won't be until 2022.

I try to be careful—everyone follows their own level of hypocrisy. My golf courses are open; I take my own electric cart unless playing with a family member. My wife and I dine, outdoors only, at our usual restaurants. Thank God we voted Trump out of office, although he still won't concede. He totally bungled the pandemic, costing hundreds of thousands of lives, tanked the economy, and divided the country along racial and political lines. The whole country is suffering from pandemic fatigue, which may eventually raise the death toll to an unfathomable number in this anticipated second wave. Thankfully, vaccines and therapeutics seem to be on the horizon.

PART III

It's spring 2021. The country has already lost more than 600,000 grandmothers, grandfathers, mothers, fathers, sisters, brothers, sons, and daughters to Covid-19. We now have three supposedly 95 percent effective vaccines—that is, if you're over sixty-five years old and lucky enough to get one. I gladly drove six hours round trip twice to Lake Worth on the east coast of Florida to get my two Moderna injections. My wife, sixty-four, just received her first Moderna vaccine shot in Miami-Dade after I filled out her medical necessity form to bypass the age restriction. Masks and social distancing are still necessary due to new, more transmissible variants from the United Kingdom, South Africa, and Brazil. Our delusional governor has declared Florida open for spring breakers, who act as if the pandemic is over. Another surge is inevitable I'm afraid.

Side note: After two months of false claims of election fraud, Trump finally left the White House but not before inciting a bloody insurrection on the Capitol that left six dead and countless injured. He leaves behind a legacy of being twice impeached and a country irrevocably divided.

Hopefully, an honest and transparent Biden administration can regain the soul of America. Godspeed to us all!

PART IV

Summer 2021 starts off in great fashion in the war against Covid-19. President Joe Biden's optimistic call to vaccinate 70 percent of all eligible Americans over the age of seventeen by July 1st falls just short, at 67 percent. Another month passes before that threshold is met. Cases, hospitalizations, and deaths all plummet to their lowest numbers since the onset of the pandemic. Surprisingly, the Centers for Disease Control and Prevention (CDC) issues an edict that fully vaccinated people no longer need to wear masks outdoors or even indoors. The Biden Build Back Better economic recovery plan takes off as the country fully reopens.

Fourth of July celebrations spring up all over the country, including the much-anticipated return of the Macy's fireworks spectacular on the East River in New York. Fans are allowed back in ballparks. I even attend a Yankees game at the stadium, seated maskless in the vaccinated section with my wife, son, and his fiancée. The pool at our New Jersey condo community finally reopens. Indoor dining at restaurants flourish. Concert tours resume. Broadway shows reopen, although Bruce Springsteen's one-man show takes the controversial but sensible stance of requiring proof of vaccination to attend. Summer camps reopen to the joy of the kids and relief of their parents.

Unfortunately, Biden has declared victory over the pandemic prematurely. By August, a fourth surge is gripping the country. The Delta variant, which devastated India and then the United Kingdom, becomes the predominant Covid strain in the US. Much more transmissible and deadlier than its predecessors, it spreads like wildfire throughout those southern and midwestern "red" states with low vaccination rates. In fact, the CDC and the administration call it the "pandemic of the unvaccinated." Not surprisingly, two Southern states with right wing Republican governors, namely Florida and Texas, account for 40 percent of the daily reported cases nationwide.

According to the CDC, previous Covid vaccination prevents 95 percent of hospitalizations and 99.9 percent of deaths from the Delta variant. However, breakthrough cases are increasing at an alarming rate. The efficacy of vaccine-induced antibodies may be waning after six months. A third booster vaccination was recently approved for immunocompromised people. Israel is already offering a booster shot for all its population over the age of sixty. At sixty-eight years old, and having been fully vaccinated early back in February, I would welcome the CDC recommendation to roll up my sleeve for a third shot.

The pandemic of the unvaccinated should never have happened in this country. Despite the Biden administration's aggressive efforts to make the vaccine available and readily accessible, 30 percent of the population refuses the vaccine. Antivaxers, Trumpers, and minorities with a well-earned suspicion of governmental health research have all created a public health fiasco. Without a federal vaccine mandate, we may never reach herd immunity.

In Florida, our Trump stooge Governor DeSantis, a self-proclaimed (vice) presidential candidate for 2024 pending Trump's decision to run again, has even prohibited mask mandates in schools. He has also threatened to withhold the salaries of all school superintendents and board members who disobey his restrictions. He misgoverns the state with the highest number of cases per day in the country (more than 20,000). He continues to play politics with public health. He is sending an army of unvaccinated children under the age of twelve, who are not yet eligible for the vaccine, back into school in late August with no masks to contract the Delta variant. These kids will then bring the virus home to their unmasked, unvaccinated parents. In a state where only 46 percent of adults are vaccinated, the hospitals are starting to be overrun with Covid cases.

It looks like my early October return to the Sunshine State will be delayed until the pandemic burns out in Florida.

PART V

Thanksgiving 2021. My wife and I are truly thankful to be joined by Margot, Stefanie, Zachary, and Betsy at our Naples home. Fully vaccinated and boosted, the CDC has deemed it safe for us to gather together in person, not on Zoom like last year.

Zach and Betsy's wedding is a go for summer 2022 in her home-town of Cincinnati. Margot has finally finished training, fourteen years post high school, and is now an assistant professor of pediatrics at Ohio State and a pediatric neuro-oncology attending at Nationwide Children's Hospital. Stefanie is in her sixth year of general surgery residency at Beth Israel Deaconess and is busy on the general surgery fellowship application tour. She would ultimately match into the two-year Surgical Critical Care and Trauma/Acute Care Surgery Fellowship at Vanderbilt University Medical Center.

Although my daughters have chosen medical careers, they couldn't be more different in temperament. Margot has a pediatrician's type B personality—patient, creative, compassionate, tolerant. Stefanie has a surgeon's type A personality—impatient, competitive, aggressive, intolerant. As the saying goes, "If you want to hide something from a surgeon—put it in the chart. If you want to hide something from an internist or pediatrician—put it under a dressing."

Still, the Covid-19 pandemic rages on. Globally, there have been 261 million documented cases to date, with 5.2 million deaths. In the United States, we are closing in on the unfathomable total of 800,000 deaths. In Florida, under the leadership of our still delusional Governor DeSantis, we have lost more than 60,000 lives to this virus. The Sunshine State ranks third in Covid fatalities behind only California and Texas. After a brutal summer Delta variant surge in Florida, the virus has finally burnt out here as expected, with a low 4 percent current positivity rate.

Inexplicably, only 70 percent of the US population has received at least one vaccine dose and only 60 percent are fully vaccinated. We now have approved vaccines for children five years old and older, but polls indicate that only 30 percent of parents plan to vaccinate their kids in the near future. With a vast supply of safe, effective vaccines administered at convenient locations, it remains inconceivable to me that the US would only rank twentieth among developed nations in share of population vaccinated. With 30 percent of our population refusing the jab, we are left vulnerable to new variants such as the Omicron South African strain, which seems to be even more transmissible than the Delta variant and perhaps more resistant to our current vaccines.

On a more positive note, prior to our annual autumnal odyssey to Florida, we checked out Zach and Betsy's new apartment. Needing more space, they moved from their one-bedroom apartment in Battery Park to a two-bedroom sublet in newly fashionable Brooklyn. Located on Bergen Street, on the border of Prospect and Crown Heights, it is a second-floor walk-up in a recently renovated eighty-year-old four-story brownstone. The neighborhood may be generously considered transitional, with numerous cafes and bars springing up to replace the previous bodegas. The apartment is fully modernized with a new kitchen and bathrooms and even has an enclosed grass backyard for a mere $4,200 per month.

As we drive around endlessly looking for a parking spot, I check my GPS and am amazed to see that the building is close to Kings County, in the heart of Crown Heights. It is only half a mile from the Brooklyn Museum, the Brooklyn Public Library, and the Brooklyn Botanical Garden. It's less than three-fourths of a mile from Grand Army Plaza, where my uncle had his surgical practice along Doctor's Row sixty years ago. Interestingly, it is within walking distance along Eastern Parkway from the Manor, where my parents were married seventy years ago.

Ironically, during all my years at the County, I never considered living in Brooklyn. Rather, I commuted 100 miles a day, and now my son lives 1.7 miles from the hospital. Forty years ago, I could have bought up all the rowhouses on his entire block for less than one million dollars and now the first-floor condo in his building sold for $1.2 million. Go figure. Who could have predicted it?

Times change; demographics shift. The 1957 departure of the Brooklyn Dodgers to Los Angeles and the replacement of Ebbets Field with public housing along Bedford Avenue signified the end of an era. White flight to the suburbs of Long Island was widespread. Over the next half century, Crown Heights saw the influx of two racially and culturally diverse populations. It now has a majority West Indian/African American population intermingled with a significant Lubavitch Hasidic Jewish community. Racial tensions have occasionally boiled over. Rapid gentrification is ongoing. In the immortal words of Bob Dylan, "The times they are a-changin'."

PART VI

August 2022. Just back from Zach and Betsy's wedding in Cincinnati. The good news—it was an action-packed weekend. Golf in the rain Friday morning at Betsy's father's rustic golf club, followed by the wedding rehearsal, and then the rehearsal dinner at Margot's favorite Cincinnati restaurant—Sotto. (The first time Margot took us to Sotto seven years ago, we saw Serena Williams and Drake in the private dining room.) Helaine and I gave speeches at the rehearsal dinner. Helaine was commended for her brevity; me not so much. Then back to our home base at the Phelps hotel for a rooftop welcome party for all the guests who had flown in from near and far. The Phelps hotel was originally constructed in 1926 by President William Taft's half-brother, Charles Phelps Taft.

Saturday was the big day. By midafternoon, it was time to start getting ready for the black-tie affair. I put on my brand-new black tuxedo and headed down to Zach's suite, where all the groomsmen were assembled. We gathered around his laptop to watch an instructional video on how to tie a bow tie. Thank goodness for YouTube. I was then summoned back upstairs to my room to help Helaine zip up her full-length gown. Why do the women in the wedding party feel obligated to spend thousands of dollars on a dress they will only wear once?

Now the bad news! Stefanie felt ill around two p.m. and tested positive for Covid. Having flown in from Boston, she would have to miss the wedding quarantined in her hotel room. I immediately took a quick antigen test, which was negative. Asymptomatic and afebrile, I decided to go on with my plans to attend the wedding. After all, most everyone else in the wedding party had recently had Covid.

By three p.m., it was time to board the party bus to the chapel, a beautiful edifice on the grounds of Betsy's old parochial all-girls high school. The interfaith ceremony conducted primarily by Deacon Rick started promptly at four p.m. One other reason I couldn't miss the ceremony—I was the designated rabbi. Helaine and I would have preferred a nondenominational setting for the wedding ceremony. We were quickly overruled by Betsy, who is Catholic, and Zach, who is currently agnostic. So, we had agreed to a ceremony jointly conducted by the deacon and a rabbi. Since Cincinnati is the birthplace of Reform Judaism, we anticipated no difficulty in finding a rabbi to officiate an interfaith wedding. Only two minor problems: Unbeknownst to me, the wedding fell on the solemn Jewish holiday of Tisha B'av. To make matters even worse, it was to be held on a Saturday afternoon before sundown during the Sabbath. So, I was thrust into the role of designated rabbi.

Thank goodness for Google. I did my online research, which guided me to three prayer selections that I conducted in Hebrew and English. I guess my parents would have been happy that my eight years of Hebrew school came in handy after all. First, I recited the Seven Blessings, followed by the Song of Solomon 6:3 vow over the wedding rings, and concluded with Zachary smashing the glass to a hearty interfaith "Mazel tov." Evidently, I was a big hit.

Then it was off by limousine to the Cincinnati Music Hall, which was a beautiful venue for the wedding reception. After that, it was all a blur as I was drinking Jameson on the rocks all night. I do remember thinking that Zach and Betsy made a beautiful couple. Their friends certainly danced up a storm.

Sunday morning was the getaway breakfast in the Phelps atrium. Then I started coughing. I retested—still negative and afebrile. I double masked on the flight back to Newark. Monday morning, I awoke with a low-grade fever and chills. I retested—faintly positive. I dragged myself to a local urgent care, which conducted a more accurate Abbott test. It was clearly positive. Being sixty-nine years old and a pipe smoker, the treating physician agreed to start me on Paxlovid, an oral antiviral, and a strong cough medicine.

It was ironic. I was double vaccinated, double boosted, and had even reverted to wearing a mask the week before the wedding. Lo and behold, I contracted Covid from of all people my daughter.

Fortunately, I had only a mild case of Covid—a low-grade fever for a day, some fatigue for a week, and a nonproductive cough for two weeks. I did not develop Paxlovid rebound, as seen in upwards of 20 percent of cases after a five-day course of the antiviral. I was back playing golf after a week. Stefanie had a slightly worse case but returned to work after a week. Surprisingly, no one we interacted with during the weekend festivities came down with Covid.

It is an indictment of the transmissibility of the Omicron BA.5 subvariant that my entire family, double vaxed and boosted, contracted Covid in the weeks before the wedding. Perhaps after two and a half years of pandemic fatigue, we have all let down our guard. We now have over 93 million reported Covid cases in the United States (not even counting all the positive home tests that were never reported) and sadly more than one million Covid deaths in this country.

Fortunately, with vaccines and boosters, antivirals, and some herd immunity, we have lowered the mortality rate of this deadly virus below 1 percent. When will it all end?

Finale

AFTER THREE-PLUS YEARS, the pandemic nightmare is officially over! The CDC ended the public health emergency on May 11, 2023, the same month it stopped reporting data on Covid cases. With the availability of at-home over-the-counter Covid-19 test kits, most positive results are never reported anyway. Rather, the CDC tracks the prevalence of Covid in a particular community with its wastewater surveillance system.

The virus hasn't disappeared; we've just learned to live with it. This summer, it seems that everyone knows a friend or family member who has contracted Covid again, albeit a fairly mild case. In November 2022, I received my bivalent booster, which targeted the Omicron subvariant XBB.1.16. In October 2023, I got the newer bivalent booster, which targets the currently prevalent Omicron subvariant EG.5—along with my flu shot. Recent published data indicates that 95 percent of the US population has circulating antibodies against Covid from prior infection or vaccination. We have finally reached herd immunity.

It's been an interesting year. But before it arrived, in December 2022, I visited my dermatologist for my annual skin surveillance session, a visit that would impact 2023. She noted a small mole on my left shoulder that required a biopsy. "No big deal. Most likely another basal cell carcinoma," she reassured me. Having had multiple basal cells removed over the years, I wasn't too concerned. The biopsy result usually takes a week. When I received a call from her nurse practitioner a mere two days later, I knew it wasn't good. To the NP's surprise, it turned out to be a malignant melanoma.

That startled me. Fortunately, my maximum Breslow thickness was only 0.4 millimeters and the final pathologic stage was T1a. With no palpable axillary lymph nodes, I didn't require a sentinel lymph node biopsy or adjuvant therapy. Two days later, I underwent a wide excision under local anesthesia. The one centimeter by one centimeter lesion required three centimeter margins in all directions down to the fascia overlying the deltoid muscle. Ultimately, that left a ten centimeter (four inch) elliptical excision to close. With aggressive undermining, the surgeon closed the wound without a skin graft. I was told to take acetaminophen for pain; no analgesic was prescribed. WTF!

I have a 99 percent five-year survival rate. In an unfortunate irony, our eight-and-a-half-year-old Goldendoodle, Harley, needed a vet with my expertise. During her annual checkup a few months after my health scare, the veterinarian noticed expansion of her upper jaw and splaying of her maxillary incisors. She was otherwise asymptomatic. We were referred to a vet who had done a dental/oral surgery three-year residency. Harley underwent a cone beam CT scan and biopsy under general anesthesia.

The diagnosis came back: fibrosarcoma of bone, evidently common in Golden Retrievers and Labrador Retrievers. The good news—fibrosarcoma in dogs rarely metastasizes. The bad news —they often recur aggressively. Without treatment, survival is six months. With resection and clear margins, survival is nine to fifteen months. We convened a family tumor board including our in-house oncologist and general surgeon. The vet/oral surgeon told us he had performed the necessary surgery multiple times with good results. I was his worst nightmare of a pet owner. I mentioned every possible complication I had ever encountered in such cases, including bleeding, infection, wound dehiscence, oronasal fistula, etc. He assured us that dogs were surprisingly stoic and tolerated the surgery well. Four of us voted to proceed with the surgery in hopes of a curative resection. Surprisingly, my daughter, the surgeon, voiced her opposition; she didn't want to subject Harley to the surgery for probable minimal gain in survival time. My wife and I made the final decision to proceed with the surgery.

The vet/oral surgeon performed a rostral partial maxillectomy including the right canine tooth to left canine tooth superiorly to the floor of the snout. Harley tolerated the surgery and long general anesthetic well. She was discharged home the same night. Her healing was complicated by severe upper lip trapping by her mandibular canine teeth. It caused traumatic ulcers of the upper soft tissue flaps that were rotated to close the maxillary defect. This necessitated a third general anesthetic to cut down the lower canines after vital pulpotomies (partial root canals). The total fee for the three surgeries: $7,500. We didn't have pet insurance. Maybe I should have been a vet oral surgeon.

Although the surgical margins were grossly negative (two centimeters), on microscopic exam one of her rostral margins was close (two millimeters). Therefore, we were referred to a veterinarian radiation oncologist for a consultation regarding adjuvant therapy. The oncologist deemed the radiation field too large for one or two stereotactic doses. He recommended nineteen fractionated radiation sessions, each requiring a brief general anesthetic. He claimed dogs tolerated the first two weeks of treatment well, but the last two weeks would take their toll—lethargy, mucositis, stomatitis, loss of appetite, etc. He was quite honest with us. Although a cure was possible, maximum survival was more likely eighteen to twenty-four months. The radiation oncology fee would be $11,000.

It wasn't the money. Harley had been lethargic and miserable for the month post-op. She was finally returning to her baseline. We reconvened our family tumor board. It was unanimous; we wouldn't torture her to extend her survival another few months. We are hoping she makes it to her tenth birthday, healthy and happy, then we'll take it day by day. One thing the pandemic has taught us is not to take anything for granted.

On a happy note, our immediate family convened in Boston the last weekend in June for Stefanie's General Surgery graduation ceremony on Sunday night. It was a beautiful affair held at the Brae Burn

Country Club in upscale Newton, home to the US Open in 1919. But first on Saturday night, it was time for my seventieth birthday dinner at a highly recommended Italian restaurant in Beacon Hill—a bit more low-key than my retirement party, but just as heartfelt. Hard to believe it had been exactly five years since I left the County.

Cheat sheet[*]

Dentistry (General Dentistry) —Profession or science dealing with the prevention and treatment of diseases and conditions of the teeth, gums, and oral cavity.

DDS versus DMD —Doctor of Dental Surgery and Doctor of Dental Medicine are equivalent based upon the university conferring the degree.

Oral Surgery —Forerunner of present-day oral and maxillofacial surgery. A branch of dentistry that dealt with the diagnosis and treatment of oral conditions requiring surgical intervention, e.g., exodontia.

Oral and Maxillofacial Surgery (OMS) —Specialty of dentistry that includes the diagnosis of diseases and surgical and adjuvant treatment of diseases, injuries, and defects involving the functional and aesthetic aspects of the hard and soft tissues of the oral cavity, face, jaws, and neck. Requires a residency of a minimum of four years post-dental school.

*unofficial definitions

OMS Resident —Four-year certificate resident. Four years of OMS residency post-dental school, including one year of off-service rotations. Graduates usually pursue private practice.

MD/OMS Resident—Six years post-dental school, includes two years of medical school with advanced standing, plus one year of general surgery internship and three years of OMS residency. Eligible for medical licensure in New York and New Jersey. Graduates often pursue advanced fellowship training, and some proceed into hospital-based practice or academia.

GPR (General Practice Resident or Residency) —One year hospital-based residency in general dentistry. Required for dental licensure in New York.

Appendix I

Glasgow Coma Scale (3-15)

<u>Eye Opening (4 points)</u>

4: Spontaneous

3: In response to speech

2: In response to pain

1: None

<u>Best Verbal Response (5 points)</u>

5: Oriented (person, place, time)

4: Confused conversation

3: Inappropriate speech

2: Incomprehensible sounds

1: None

<u>Best Motor Response (6 points)</u>

6: Obeys commands

5: Localizes to pain

4: Withdraws to pain

3: Flexor response to pain

2: Extensor response to pain

1: No response to pain

GCS 3-8 = Severe Head Injury

Appendix II

LeFort Fractures

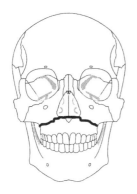

LEFORT I FRACTURE
horizontal fracture

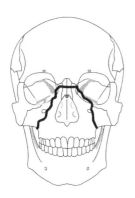

LEFORT II FRACTURE
pyramidal fracture

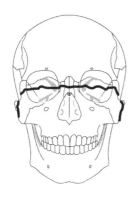

LEFORT III FRACTURE
craniofacial disjunction

Appendix III
Parting Shots/Patient Pearls

Purpose of this visit. "To see the dinst." "Tooth decade." (dentist/decay)

"I'm not the husband *per se*. I'm the spouse."

NPO—nothing to eat or drink after midnight. "Man, I'm gonna be one dry-assed motherfucker."

You ever have heart disease? "Yep, my heart attacked me once."

Take any antibiotics? "Senipilliums so's I don't get the Smilin' Mighty Jesus." (penicillin/spinal meningitis)

Are you diabetic? "I'm not sure, but I take insulation cause my panogrease ain't working too good." (insulin/pancreas)

On the medical questionnaire: Do you currently have any infections? "Near to the pussy."

Prior to a general anesthetic: Sir, did you have anything to eat or drink since midnight? "Doc, the only thing been in my mouth since last night was my wife's titty."

Young lady inquired post extraction: "I know I can drink when I get home, but when can I perform . . . ?" "Well, sucking through a straw can give you a dry socket, so you figure it out."

Bonus: One of our totally institutionalized female residents responds to a whining post-op fracture patient who wants his IMF (jaws wired shut) released early AMA (against medical advice). "Man up, and grow a pair of balls."

Acknowledgment

SPECIAL THANKS TO Dr. Steven Izzo, associate OMS program director, for helping me with things I had forgotten along the way.

Thanks to my daughter Stefanie for her help with manuscript editing and preparation.

Thanks to the whole staff at Koehler Books for taking on this project including: John Koehler, publisher, Joe Coccaro, executive editor, and Danielle Koehler, design director.

Milton Keynes UK
Ingram Content Group UK Ltd.
UKHW011140220424
441551UK00007B/707